NO MORE DRAMA!

RELATIONSHIPS

OVERCOMING THE
INSANITY OF DRAMA
IN RELATIONSHIPS

WIL & GRACE NICHOLS

No More Drama! Relationships
Copyright © 2009 by Wil Nichols

Request for information should be addressed to:
More Than Conquerors Publishing
PO Box 14392, Research Triangle Park, North Carolina 27709

ISBN 978-0-9824144-0-8

Cover Design: Algenon Conyers/Visionary Designz
www.visionarydesignz.com

Printing in the United States of America
First Edition, 2009

Special Thanks

We want to give special thanks to the people in our lives that have truly been a blessing to us!

Our Personal Family: Crystal, our Daughter and Anthony, our Son; our parents, brothers, sisters, and the rest of you all!

Our Spiritual Family: All of our brothers, sisters, sons, and daughters of Victorious Praise Fellowship Church; and all the church families and brothers and sisters in Christ who have been a part of our lives over the years.

Contents

Introduction

A lifelong friendship that should have formed a partnership that would birth a successful multimillion dollar business ends because of the drama of gossip. A marriage made in heaven, that should have raised a son who would be the next president of the United States, ends because of the drama of betrayal and broken trust. A ministry that was on its way to being a mega-church which would have been a blessing to an impoverished community is torn apart because of the drama of sexual misconduct.

Everybody at some level deals with drama; the drama of marital discord that leads to separation and divorce; the drama of the workplace that leads to people quitting or being fired; the drama of families that leads to family members not speaking to each other for years; or the drama of relationships that leads to the breakup of lifelong friendships. Drama impacts every area of our lives, and prevents us from achieving the purpose of our existence. It prevents us because it destroys the relationships that were designed to bring that purpose to pass.

Lives, businesses, careers, and even ministries are being destroyed everyday because of drama. And when you look at what's left in its wake, one must conclude that drama is no laughing matter. Families destroyed, reputations shattered, severe depression, missed opportunities, loss of faith and trust, broken promises, financial ruin, emotional distress, and even suicide are just a few of the consequences of drama. These consequences tell us that not only is drama nothing to play with but, that there must be more to it than meets the natural eye; that there must a spiritual component that goes beyond the natural issues we see.

One of the experiences that Jesus had during His ministry is recorded in the Gospel of Mark, the 5th chapter, verses 1-9. There He meets a man who is described as having an unclean spirit. This man was unable to cope with societal norms, in constant torment, living in a grave yard, completely out of control, cutting himself with stones, going in and out of sanity, a danger to both himself and those around him. When Jesus asked him his name, he said, "My name is Legion: for we are many." A legion during the time of Jesus was the principle unit of the Roman army which consisted of about 6826 men. In layman's terms, this man was struggling with nearly seven thousand unclean spirits. Later we will explore in greater detail how this man got to this place, but from the study of demonology we learn that these spirits were fallen angels that were kicked out of heaven with Lucifer or Satan when he attempted to lift himself above the throne of God. Their mission was to kill, steal, and to destroy the Kingdom of Heaven; to bring discord, devastation, and destruction to the earth and to the lives of the people of God. This sounds exactly like the consequences of drama.

Drama is not just the lurid details of a broken home, a destroyed ministry, or someone's shattered reputation that we find ourselves reading or talking about, but it is about the forces behind the drama that are violently destroying our lives and God's purpose. These forces are spiritual, and therefore impact our soul (mind, will, and emotions) at the spiritual level. The Bible teaches us in Ephesians the 6th chapter and 12th verse that these forces comprise a kingdom of four different levels: Principalities, Powers, Rulers of the Darkness, and Spiritual Wickedness. Each of these levels of unclean spirits in turn are behind four different types of drama: Personal, Territorial, Temptation, and Spiritual.

Our goal should be to live a "Drama Free" lifestyle. The only way to do this is to learn how to combat the drama that we face every day. This will only occur when we learn what we are dealing with, the forces behind it, and the strategies, both natural and spiritual, necessary to defeat it. When we do this, living a life of "No More Drama" will not just be our goal, but the reality that God intended for us when He created, called, and ordained us for His purpose.

PART 1: Overcoming The Insanity Of Relationships

The Four Stages of Drama

In the Introduction, we stated that "Drama" is more than "the details of broken homes or shattered reputations." It is also more than the frustrating back and forth struggles we find ourselves engaging in with co-workers, church members, neighbors, and our spouses. With the number of broken homes, destroyed marriages, hurt and abused church members, and shattered friendships; drama is not simply just about disagreements and arguments, but it is about devices used by satanic forces.

2 Corinthians 2:11 (KJV) [11]Lest Satan should get an advantage of us: for we are not ignorant of his devices.

When we fight, argue, get engaged in territorial disputes, deal with hurt and betrayal, or struggle with church hurt and abuse; we must understand that these are all various forms of devices used by Satan and his organized forces. Forces we are commanded to stand against.

Ephesians 6:10-12 (KJV) [10]Finally, my brethren, be strong in the Lord, and in the power of his might. [11]Put on the whole armour of God that ye may be able to stand against the wiles of the devil. [12]For we wrestle not against flesh and blood, but against principalities, against powers, against the rulers of the darkness of this world, against spiritual wickedness in high places.

As discussed, the enemy has organized his forces into four categories; Principalities, Powers, Rulers of Darkness, and Spiritual Wickedness.

"Principalities" are the demonic forces that have the oversight over territories, jurisdictions, and correspond to the rank of generals. They produce what is called "Territorial Drama". This is the drama of territorial spirits that fight you when they are threatened when you move into what they consider to be their territory. They also produce the drama of controlling spirits when they try to control the relationships of others.

"Powers" represent various levels of foot soldiers. They would be considered the privates of the demonic world that attack at the individual or personal level and produce what is called "Personal Drama". This is the drama of personal attacks and destruction, victimizing people by using their personal failures and weaknesses to Satan's influence.

"Rulers of the Darkness of this World" are the demonic forces that have charge over Satan's worldly businesses, namely the things of the world that bring temptation. They produce what is called "Temptation Drama". This drama comes about as a result of the lust of the flesh, lust of the eyes, and the pride of life.

"Spiritual Wickedness in High Places" are demonic forces that have charge over religion and operate in the church. They produce what is called "Spiritual Drama". This is the drama that stems from church hurt from lay members and spiritual abuse by church leaders.

If we are to develop a lifestyle of "No More Drama", we must understand each level of drama, and develop strategies on how to deal with them. The drama in our homes, marriages, and friendships is different from the drama of the world and its temptations. The drama of the workplace and marketplace is different from the drama of the religion and the church world. If we are to keep Satan from getting an advantage over our lives, it is imperative that we take a four tiered approach to dealing with drama. The chapters that follow look at each of these stages of drama, how they destroy relationships, and how to combat them to become "Drama Free"!

The Making Of A "Drama Queen / King"

We all know of at least one "Drama Queen" or "Drama King"; an individual that appears to be filled with drama. They are always involved with drama at some level, either receiving drama or giving drama. Whenever you see them coming or see their number on the caller-id, you know that there is going to be drama. They engage in all types of drama; dramas of personal attacks, territorial drama with new people. Drama Queens and Drama Kings are constantly falling prey to the temptation of drama, or always involved in church drama. The question we must ask is; how do they get to the point of always being associated and affiliated with drama?

Based on the premise that drama is a device of demonic forces and unclean spirits of Satan's kingdom; let's look at a person who may have been one of the biggest "Drama Kings" of the Bible. Mark the 5th chapter tells us about a man that Jesus met who said his name was "Legion!"

Mark 5:1-5 (KJV) ¹And they came over unto the other side of the sea, into the country of the Gadarenes. ²And when he was come out of the ship, immediately there met him out of the tombs a man with an unclean spirit, ³Who had his dwelling among the tombs; and no man could bind him, no, not with chains: ⁴Because that he had been often bound with *fetters and chains, and the chains had been plucked asunder by him, and the fetters broken in pieces: neither could any man tame him. ⁵And always, night and day, he was in the mountains, and in the tombs, crying, and cutting himself with stones.*

Mark 5:9 (KJV) ⁹And he asked him, what is thy name? And he answered, saying, my name is Legion: for we are many.

This uncontrollable man, breaking chains and shackles at will, was filled with a legion of demons. Again, a legion during this period represented nearly seven thousand men. In this case he was filled with almost seven thousand demons and their associated drama. He had to be the personification of drama; going in and out of insanity, living in a graveyard, crying day and night, and engaging in self mutilation by cutting himself. So how did he get to this state?

Matthew 12:43-45 (KJV) ⁴³When the unclean spirit is gone out of a man, he walketh through dry places, seeking rest, and findeth none. ⁴⁴Then he saith, I will return into my house from whence I came out; and when he is come, he findeth it empty, swept, and garnished. ⁴⁵Then goeth he, and taketh with himself seven other spirits more wicked than himself, and they enter in and dwell there: and the last state of that man is worse than the first. Even so shall it be also unto this wicked generation.

There are several things we learn from this passage, the first being that the level of drama increases generationally. Generationally can be defined through a person's actions, that is, doing the same thing over and over (which is also a form of insanity when you expect to get different results) or through birth. This passage shows us that every time a spirit leaves and comes back, it comes back with seven more spirits, more wicked then himself. Each generation grows by a factor of seven. He goes from one demon to seven, seven to forty nine, forty nine to over three hundred, three hundred to over two thousand; and so on. We get to a point where he has a legion of demons inside of him.

Psalm 51:5 (KJV) [5]Behold, I was shapen in iniquity; and in sin did my mother conceive me.

This passage of scripture tells us that we start out conceived in sin (which is our first generation) then we go through life being shaped and formed as a result of our experiences. The more experiences a person has that are associated with drama, the worse they become. Thus, we end up with a "Drama Queen or King"!

The good news is that regardless of how a person gets to that state or even how bad the state is, there is a solution.

Mark 5:13-15 (KJV) [13]And forthwith Jesus gave them leave. And the unclean spirits went out, and entered into the swine: and the herd ran violently down a steep place into the sea, (they were about two thousand;) and were choked in the sea. [14]And they that fed the swine fled, and told it in the city, and in the country. And they went out to see what it was that was done. [15]And they come to Jesus, and see him that was possessed with the devil, and had the legion, sitting, and clothed, and in his right mind: and they were afraid.

The Power To Choose

Most of the drama we experience comes from inter-personal relationships. It is these close personal relationships that cause most of our hurt, frustration, betrayal, and depression. We become angry, anger turns to bitterness, and bitterness becomes wrath (vengeful retribution). Close friendships, committed relationships, and marriages produce more drama than anything else in our lives because of the emotions involved in these relationship.

Our dilemma is that we need relationships to survive and fulfill our purpose. We were not created as solitary creatures expected to go through life by ourselves. But we were created in the image of God and everything God did was done in relationship:

Genesis 1:26 (KJV) [26] And God said, Let us make man in our image, after our likeness: and let them have dominion over the fish of the sea, and over the fowl of the air, and over the cattle, and over all the earth, and over every creeping thing that creepeth upon the earth.

John 1:1-3 (KJV) [1] In the beginning was the Word and the Word was with God, and the Word was God. [2] The same was in the beginning with God. [3] All things were made by him; and without him was not any thing made that was made.

Everything about us requires relationships. Our vision requires relationships because we need people ready to run with it as the provision for the vision:

Habakkuk 2:2 (KJV) ²*And the LORD answered me, and said, Write the vision, and make it plain upon tables, that he may run that readeth it.*

Our mission requires relationships because we are called to be witnesses:

Acts 1:8 (KJV) ⁸*But ye shall receive power, after that the Holy Ghost is come upon you: and ye shall be witnesses unto me both in Jerusalem, and in all Judaea, and in Samaria, and unto the uttermost part of the earth.*

Our purpose requires relationships because we are here to be a blessing to others:

Jeremiah 1:5 (KJV) ⁵*Before I formed thee in the belly I knew thee; and before thou camest forth out of the womb I sanctified thee, and I ordained thee a prophet unto the nations.*

Even our salvation requires relationships because we can't keep the commandments of our Lord and Savior without them:

Matthew 22:36-40 (KJV) ³⁶*Master, which is the great commandment in the law?* ³⁷*Jesus said unto him,*

Thou shalt love the Lord thy God with all thy heart, and with all thy soul, and with all thy mind. [38]This is the first and great commandment. [39]And the second is like unto it, Thou shalt love thy neighbour as thyself. [40]On these two commandments hang all the law and the prophets.

Relationships start on a very personal one-on-one level between two people; two business partners, two co-workers, two best friends, two family members, two church members, or even a husband and wife. Regardless of what type of relationship it is, every relationship has the potential to take one of two different paths.

Two married couples: one is twenty years into spending the rest of their lives together while the other is in divorce court fighting over pots and pans.

Two professional women in Corporate America: one is rejoicing over her third promotion in a year, the other one just stormed out, cursing everybody out.

Two church members: one has accepted Christ, experienced spiritual growth, and working in ministry while the other has backslid and left the church.

What is it that leads one relationship to end in disaster and another to succeed? Yes, drama is the instigating factor, but all relationships have drama.

The answer is the choices people make when the drama shows up.

Deuteronomy 30:15 (KJV) *15See, I have set before thee this day life and good, and death and evil;*

Deuteronomy 30:19 (KJV) *19I call heaven and earth to record this day against you, that I have set before you life and death, blessing and cursing: therefore choose life, that both thou and thy seed may live:*

Joshua 24:15 (KJV) *15And if it seem evil unto you to serve the LORD, choose you this day whom ye will serve; whether the gods which your fathers served that were on the other side of the flood, or the gods of the Amorites, in whose land ye dwell: but as for me and my house, we will serve the LORD.*

The problem with the choices that we make is the helplessness we feel in making them. We don't want to fight, yet we fight. We don't intend to hurt, yet we hurt. It's not our intent to react with anger, yet we find ourselves constantly fighting.

Romans 7:21 (KJV) *21I find then a law, that, when I would do good, evil is present with me.*

The reality of this good and evil in all of us comes both from our heritage and our environment. David described the evil in us:

Psalm 51:5 (KJV) ⁵Behold, I was shapen in iniquity; and in sin did my mother conceive me.

This passage reveals that generational and environmental forces, internal and external pressures form and shape our cognitive thinking, emotional feelings, and reactionary behaviors.

Romans 7:19 (KJV) ¹⁹For the good that I would I do not: but the evil which I would not, that I do.

Sometimes we feel like we are slaves to thoughts and emotions. The choices that we make in our relationships can depend on when you catch us. We are like the Almond Joy candy bar, "Sometimes you feel like a nut, sometimes you don't." We feel helpless to what's in us and what's around us.

The Holy Spirit gives us authority over our choices; the power to live life not predicated or dictated by the drama in our lives or others, but according to the power of God.

Choose Better Not Bitter

The experiences of relationships will either make us better or they will make us bitter. We have the power to choose which. Our soul is like a sponge that soaks up water. Since our soul is our mind, will, and emotions, over time we soak in thoughts, feelings, and behaviors and ultimately they become us. We end up having thoughts like: "I don't know why I'm thinking this way!"; "I can't help how I feel!"; "I don't know why I keep doing this!"

Have you ever set out to drive one place and end up going somewhere else? The somewhere else is what has been built up in you. At an emotional and spiritual level, what builds up in us are the experiences we have soaked up from past relationships.

When people hurt us, that hurt builds up in us. When they disappoint, frustrate, anger, or aggravate us; all those things build up in us. We become disappointed, frustrated, angry, and aggravated. Over time this buildup becomes bitterness. That bitterness has set in because you develop a spirit of apathy, hopelessness, and faithlessness. You simply give up on relationships all together; you stop using your sponge. The problem is that the sponge was created to absorb, clean, and wash, while we were created to be in a relationship.

We must not allow the mess to make us bitter, but choose to become better and rinse out the sponge with clean water. When we go in and out of relationships, we must not allow the mess of others to make us bitter, but use it as an opportunity to become better.

James 1:2-4 (KJV) ²My brethren, count it all joy when ye fall into divers temptations; ³Knowing this, that the trying of your faith worketh patience. ⁴But let patience have her perfect work, that ye may be perfect and entire, wanting nothing.

We must become like a "good fireman"! What makes a good fireman? Not one with a unsoiled suit, a clean truck, or an unused water hose, but one that smells like smoke, with a truck that has soot all over it, and worn, beat up water hoses. Why? Because he's been in the fire! Not only has he been in the fire, he's learned how to come through the fire.

1 Peter 1:7 (KJV) ⁷That the trial of your faith, being much more precious than of gold that perisheth, though it be tried with fire, might be found unto praise and honour and glory at the appearing of Jesus Christ:

A good husband is a man who feels like he's married to the devil wearing a wig, but he hangs in there anyway. A good wife is the woman who feels like I may not be married to the worse husband in the world, but until they find him, her husband will do.

What makes a good church member is not a good church with good members, but someone who can put up with church drama kings and queens, get hurt and disappointed, and still praise God. These are people who have chosen to become better from their relationships, not bitter.

Choose to "Turn To" so you don't "Turn On"

Most people enter into relationships with a theoretical desire to help each other. In marriage, couples vow "for better or for worse." Theoretically, they form a covenant relationship based on God's love; a bond that cannot be broken, held together by a love that never fails. They form relationships with a desire to turn to each other in times of trouble.

In reality all they form is a symbiotic relationship based on human love; a bond that is based on human affection that can be easily broken because there's a thin line between love and hate. When drama hits, instead of them turning to each other, they turn on each other!

Symbiotic relationships are based on receiving, and so people in these relationships give what they receive. Whereas a covenant relationship is based on giving, and so people in these relationships give in spite of what they receive.

Relationships that start out singing, "ain't no mountain high enough, ain't no river wide enough, ain't no valley low enough to keep me from you" are now singing a different song. Now they are saying "Come on Cletus, Come on! You gone walk over here, but you're gone limp back." We're trying to turn to each other, but we end up turning on each other. "I can't stand you, I hate you, I wish I would have never met you", become the language that we speak as we turn on each other.

The reason we turn on each other is because we are turning to the wrong thing. When we turn to people, we end up disappointed because people fail us. Before we know it, we turn on them.

Psalm 146:3 (KJV) ³Put not your trust in princes, nor in the son of man, in whom there is no help.

People will hurt us, disappoint us, betray us, and even curse us. When we feel that they have turned on us, this creates a response of us turning on them.

Turn the other cheek sounds good; do good to them that despitefully misuse you also sounds good; but the reality is we want to hurt them, curse them, and fight back. We become the embodiment of Paul's letter to the Romans:

Romans 7:21 (KJV) [21]I find then a law, that, when I would do good, evil is present with me.

Romans 7:24 (KJV) [24]O wretched man that I am! Who shall deliver me from the body of this death?

Since people will fail us, we must stop turning to them as our source. We must to turn to God and trust in Him.

Psalm 7:1 (KJV) [1]O LORD my God, in thee do I put my trust: save me from all them that persecute me, and deliver me:

Psalm 46:1 (KJV) [1]God is our refuge and strength, a very present help in trouble.

2 Chronicles 7:14 (KJV) [14]If my people, which are called by my name, shall humble themselves, and pray, and seek my face, and turn from their wicked ways; then will I hear from heaven, and will forgive their sin, and will heal their land.

Psalm 27:1-5 (KJV) [1]The LORD is my light and my salvation; whom shall I fear? The LORD is the strength of my life; of whom shall I be afraid? [2]When the wicked, even mine enemies and my foes, came upon me to eat up my flesh, they stumbled and fell. [3]Though an host should encamp against me, my heart shall not fear: though war should rise against me, in this will I be confident. [4]One thing have I desired of the LORD, that will I seek after; that I may dwell in the house of the LORD all the days of my life, to behold the beauty of the LORD, and to enquire in his temple. ⁵For in the time of trouble he shall hide me in his pavilion: in the secret of his tabernacle shall he hide me; he shall set me up upon a rock.

With God we can live out Romans 12:21, "Be not overcome of evil, but overcome evil with good." Why? Because God is good, and since God is in us, we don't return evil, we overcome it with the God that is in us.

When we make a choice to turn to God, He keeps us from turning on each other. People may turn on us, but with God we can choose not turn on them.

Choose to be Powerful and not Powerless

The devil has been trying to keep us powerless all our lives. A slave to our desires, a slave to our flesh, a slave to sin, a slave to people, a slave to our hurts, bitterness, anger, and hatred. We must decide to stop being a slave, to stop being powerless.

2 Corinthians 5:17 (KJV) ¹⁷Therefore if any man be in Christ, he is a new creature: old things are passed away; behold, all things are become new.

We may have been born a slave but we were reborn the master. We were born defeated, but we were reborn more than a conqueror. We were born a day late and a dollar short, but reborn with the blessings of the Lord that make us rich. We were born hated among men, but reborn with the love of God. We were born depressed and weak, but reborn with the joy of the Lord. We were born powerless, but we were reborn powerful.

John 10:17-18 (KJV) [17]Therefore doth my Father love me, because I lay down my life, that I might take it again. [18]No man taketh it from me, but I lay it down of myself. I have power to lay it down, and I have power to take it again. This commandment have I received of my Father.

Luke 10:19 (KJV) [19]Behold, I give unto you power to tread on serpents and scorpions, and over all the power of the enemy: and nothing shall by any means hurt you.

We are not taking the mess of relationships, the lies, mistreatment, hatred, or betrayal because we're weak. We take them because when we are weak in the flesh, then are we strong in the spirit. We chose to be powerful by choosing the power of God.

Matthew 10:1 (KJV) [1]And when he had called unto him his twelve disciples, he gave them power against unclean spirits, to cast them out, and to heal all manner of sickness and all manner of disease.

If God Don't Do It (Personal Drama)

Most of our relationships are of a personal one-on-one nature. These relationships are important because they are the basis our existence: why we were called. It is through relationships that our vision, mission, purpose, and even our commandment to love will be fulfilled.

The flip side of the coin called relationships is the drama and hell people put us through. Satan has assigned powers to each of our relationships with the purpose of destroying them.

Ephesians 6:12 (KJV) *¹²For we wrestle not against flesh and blood, but against principalities, against powers, against the rulers of the darkness of this world, against spiritual wickedness in high places.*

Since most of our relationships are personal, most of Satan's forces are powers; that is unclean spirits that attack us at a personal level. Let's again look at the story of the man that was possessed with over a legion of demons:

Mark 5:1-9 (KJV) *¹And they came over unto the other side of the sea, into the country of the Gadarenes.* *²And when he was come out of the ship, immediately there met him out of the tombs a man with an unclean spirit,* *³Who had his dwelling among the tombs; and no man could bind him, no, not with chains: ⁴Because that he had been often bound with fetters and chains, and the chains had been plucked asunder by him, and the fetters broken in pieces: neither could any man tame him. ⁵And always, night and day, he was in the mountains, and in the tombs, crying, and cutting himself with stones. ⁶But when he saw Jesus afar off, he ran and worshipped him, ⁷And cried with a loud voice, and said, What have I to do with thee, Jesus, thou Son of the most high God? I adjure thee by God, that thou torment me not. ⁸For he said unto him, Come out of the man, thou unclean spirit. ⁹And he asked him, what is thy name? And he answered, saying, my name is Legion: for we are many.*

When Jesus asked the possessed man his name he answered "Legion, for we are many!" Legion was a body of soldiers whose number consisted of about 6826 men; 6100 were foot soldiers or personal powers. These powers attack us personally, by attaching themselves to the personalities of people around us. They pervert and distort those personalities into domination, intimidation, manipulation, and instigation, creating personality disorders.

They attack us with personal destruction, creating drama that brings us hurt, anger, bitterness, depression, frustration, and even wrath and vengeance. This drama not only impacts current relationships, but has a residual effect on future ones before they are even formed; creating a living hell trying to navigate through personal drama mind fields.

We struggle, we cry, we fight, we cry some more, we reason, we cry some more, we try to figure it out, ask others for help, get counseling, and cry some more. Eventually we learn, it's going to take the power of God to defeat the forces behind these personal attacks so that we can fulfill the purpose in which God formed our relationships!

No Longer A Victim Of Their Failures

"They Just Don't Do It For Me!"

The first issue we deal with concerning the drama of powers in relationships is the disillusionment of unrealized or unfulfilled needs. Every individual has a set of needs, some of them are innate or inherent needs based on one's DNA when they are born. Others are needs that were nurtured or formed in us based on our environment or surroundings.

Some needs are physical, psychological, and spiritual. Drama enters the picture when these needs are not met.

The drama from unmet needs are illustrated by babies. Some babies cry when they are wet, but when you change them, they stop. Some babies cry when they are hungry, but when you feed them, they stop. Some babies cry when they are lonely, but when you hold them, they stop. The point is that the crying and the drama, comes because the baby has unfulfilled needs.

The same is true with husbands and wives, backstabbing co-workers, church members about to kill each other, and families falling apart. We all have needs that are not being fulfilled, so we cry. It is a cry for help saying that I want you to fulfill my needs. So, what do you do when who you're crying to is incapable of meeting your need?

People start out with ability; the power to do a thing. Unexercised ability becomes capability; the potential to do a thing. Then unrealized potential becomes incapability, powerlessness, and failure. Therefore it is not that they don't do it for us, nor is it that they won't do it for us, it is that they are in a state where they "CAN'T" do it for us.

When people don't meet our needs, it's not our fault, it's their failure; and we need to stop being a victim of the failures of others. We become a victim of their failures when we allow their failures to make us mad or cause us resentment, hurt and bitterness. We must understand that their failure is not our fault. We must refuse to be their victim.

God asked Cain, where is your brother, he said, Am I my brother's keeper? He said that knowing that he had just killed his brother. People know when they have hurt you, talked about you, lied on you, or betrayed you. But God didn't ask Cain, are you your brother's keeper. Why? Because he wasn't! There is only one keeper, and His name is Jesus. He is the one and only person capable of being the keeper of us all.

People can't supply all our needs, but God can:

Philippians 4:19 (KJV) [19]But my God shall supply all your need according to his riches in glory by Christ Jesus.

People can't bring you peace, but God can:

Isaiah 26:3 (KJV) [3]Thou wilt keep him in perfect peace, whose mind is stayed on thee: because he trusteth in thee.

People can't make you happy, but God can bring you joy:

Nehemiah 8:10 (KJV) [10]Then he said unto them, Go your way, eat the fat, and drink the sweet, and send portions unto them for whom nothing is prepared: for this day is holy unto our Lord: neither be ye sorry; for the joy of the LORD is your strength.

Paul described to us a relationship that has moved beyond the struggles of personal drama and of unfulfilled needs in his letter to the Philippians. He stated that "I rejoice in the fact that you look to satisfy my needs", but he wanted them to know that he has learned how to be content even when they couldn't satisfy him. He was content because he knew that his God would supply all his needs.

Philippians 4:10-13 (KJV) [10]But I rejoiced in the Lord greatly, that now at the last your care of me hath flourished again; wherein ye were also careful, but ye lacked opportunity. [11]Not that I speak in respect of want: for I have learned, in whatsoever state I am, therewith to be content. [12]I know both how to be abased, and I know how to abound: every where and in all things I am instructed both to be full and to be hungry, both to abound and to suffer need. [13]I can do all things through Christ which strengtheneth me.

Philippians 4:19 (KJV) [19]But my God shall supply all your need according to his riches in glory by Christ Jesus.

No Longer A Victim Of Their Weaknesses

"They Just Won't Stop Doing It To Me!"

The second issue concerning the Drama of Powers is not about "what they don't do for me", it's about "what they keep doing to me". "For me" deals with our needs and can bring about frustration, but "to me" deals with their needs, and can bring about anger and wrath.

The first issue dealt with emotions. This issue deals with behaviors. It is very personal, dealing with personalities. This drama focuses more on their wants vs. your needs. They attack you because of what they want and what they want is what they see in you. Even if they can't get it, they will attack you to keep you from having it.

2 Corinthians 5:17 (KJV) ¹⁷Therefore if any man be in Christ, he is a new creature: old things are passed away; behold, all things are become new.

This explains why people can be with you for years, and then all of a sudden turn and attack you! When God anoints you, the old you passes away, and a new you is birthed with purpose and destiny. Instead of them trying to find out what God wants them to do, they attack you for what He's called you to do. If we are not careful, their attacks will affect our anointing.

Why? Because we take what they are doing personally!

The closest thing you have to you is you and when someone attacks you, it is human nature for you to take it personally. If you take what they did personally, you will personally attack back. Two things you must remember in order to defeat the Drama of Powers: 1) They can't help it and 2) It ain't personal!

First of all, people who are influenced by powers will do things to us because "they can't help it!" The reason why they won't stop is because they can't stop!

John 8:44 (KJV) *⁴⁴Ye are of your father the devil, and the lusts of your father ye will do. He was a murderer from the beginning, and abode not in the truth, because there is no truth in him. When he speaketh a lie, he speaketh of his own: for he is a liar, and the father of it.*

John 15:25 (KJV) *²⁵But this cometh to pass, that the word might be fulfilled that is written in their law, They hated me without a cause.*

Psalm 69:4 (KJV) *⁴They that hate me without a cause are more than the hairs of mine head: they that would destroy me, being mine enemies wrongfully, are mighty: then I restored that which I took not away.*

The second thing we must remember about people when they attack us is that it is not personal. They are not attacking us; instead they are attacking the God that is in us.

1 Samuel 8:7 (KJV) ⁷And the LORD said unto Samuel, Hearken unto the voice of the people in all that they say unto thee: for they have not rejected thee, but they have rejected me, that I should not reign over them.

When people reject us, it's not about us; it's about the anointing, the purpose, and the destiny that God has placed in us. If it's not about us, then we need to stop worrying about it and trying to fix it.

Romans 12:19 (KJV) ¹⁹Dearly beloved, avenge not yourselves, but rather give place unto wrath: for it is written, Vengeance is mine; I will repay, saith the Lord.

Romans 12:21 (KJV) ²¹Be not overcome of evil, but overcome evil with good.

They attack us because of their weakness to the evil in them, but we leave it to God because of the strength of God's power and God's goodness in us.

1 John 4:4 (KJV) ⁴Ye are of God, little children, and have overcome them: because greater is he that is in you, than he that is in the world.

There's a point when we must recognize that the problem is not about us, but about their weakness. When we do, we stop being a victim of the weaknesses of others. If they were stronger, then they wouldn't be doing what they are doing. Since they are not, don't take it personal, they just can't help it!

Victory Will Happen Through Me!

Victory is not because of me, but because of what God is doing through me.

Philippians 1:21 (KJV) ²¹For to me to live is Christ, and to die is gain.

Galatians 2:20 (KJV) ²⁰I am crucified with Christ: nevertheless I live; yet not I, but Christ liveth in me: and the life which I now live in the flesh I live by the faith of the Son of God, who loved me, and gave himself for me.

Victory means refusing to be a victim any longer. It is saying to one's self, "I'm no longer a victim of my needs." People don't meet our needs because they can't meet our needs. They are weak and being controlled by their father the devil. They hate without a cause, so leave it alone because it's not about us, but about the God in us. They didn't reject us they rejected the God in us. They didn't leave us they left the God in us. They didn't betray us they betrayed the God in us. Now if God is in us, we can rejoice because that means that victory is in us!

Philippians 4:19 (KJV) [19]But my God shall supply all your need according to his riches in glory by Christ Jesus.

2 Corinthians 2:14 (KJV) [14]Now thanks be unto God, which always causeth us to triumph in Christ, and maketh manifest the savour of his knowledge by us in every place.

Philippians 1:6 (KJV) [6]Being confident of this very thing, that he which hath begun a good work in you will perform it until the day of Jesus Christ:

Stand Your Ground (Territorial Drama)

The next type of drama we want to deal with is the drama that is produced by principalities. These unclean spirits are like generals who have charge over territories and produce territorial drama.

Ephesians 6:12 (KJV) ¹²For we wrestle not against flesh and blood, but against principalities, against powers, against the rulers of the darkness of this world, against spiritual wickedness in high places.

They affect entire territories or regions with spirits such as crime, violence, poverty, depression, separation, divorce, fornication and other sexual sins. Regardless of the sin, they all have one thing in common, a controlling territorial spirit.

Matthew 8:28 (KJV) ²⁸And when he was come to the other side into the country of the Gergesenes, there met him two possessed with devils, coming out of the tombs, exceeding fierce, so that no man might pass by that way.

Perhaps you have had experiences where you ran into someone who became very territorial; a new job, new church or even a ministry within the church. Maybe you have had people come into your territory or relationship and try to control it. Principalities are responsible for these controlling spirits. They invade your territory to take over and control what you have. They also attack you when God advances and expands your territory. Their goal is to control what you have and what God is giving you. Since everything about us (vision, mission, calling, and purpose) is about relationships; their ultimate purpose is to move in, control, and create drama that is ultimately designed to destroy the relationships associated with these territories.

The key to dealing with principalities or territorial spirits is to stand up to them.

Ephesians 6:11 (KJV) *[11]Put on the whole armour of God, that ye may be able to stand against the wiles of the devil.*

Matthew 11:12 (NLT) *[12]And from the time John the Baptist began preaching and baptizing until now, the Kingdom of Heaven has been forcefully advancing, and violent people attack it.*

The enemy is counting on us to run, quit, and give up, but God is calling on us to stand our ground, refuse to give up what we have and to advance into what He's giving us.

Stand Up To The Invaders

Invaders are the territorial spirits that invade the territory of others with the goal of raiding, looting, and pillaging everything that they can. They are marauders who roam the land looking for the good territory that others have taken the time to develop and nurture. They don't work their own territory; they simply take what others have already worked. Once they invade a territory, they become like locusts, bringing destruction to everything in their path until there is nothing left and then they move on.

Every relationship that God has ordained in our lives is a territory with a purpose. This purpose comes from God and works together for the good of them that love Him. The enemy assigns territorial spirits that invade the territory of our relationships to plunder and loot them. They invade our marriages to turn husband against wife; they invade families to turn brother against sister; they invade friendships to turn friend against friend; and they invade ministries and churches to turn member against member. Once the territory is ravished and the relationship is destroyed, they move on, leaving the territory in desolation.

If we are to protect our territory and fulfill our purpose and destiny, we must learn to keep the invaders out. Our marriages have too many invaders in them; outside influences negatively impacting the bond between a man and a woman. Our ministry and churches have too many invaders; folks that are always giving us all the latest gossip against our brothers and sisters. Our friendships have too many invaders; people that don't even know you, turning you against someone you've known all your life.

So why do they invade? They invade because there is value in our territory and they want it.

Isaiah 54:1-5 (KJV) [1]Sing, O barren, thou that didst not bear; break forth into singing, and cry aloud, thou that didst not travail with child: for more are the children of the desolate than the children of the married wife, saith the LORD. [2]Enlarge the place of thy tent, and let them stretch forth the curtains of thine habitations: spare not, lengthen thy cords, and strengthen thy stakes; [3]For thou shalt break forth on the right hand and on the left; and thy seed shall inherit the Gentiles, and make the desolate cities to be inhabited. [4]Fear not; for thou shalt not be ashamed: neither be thou confounded; for thou shalt not be put to shame: for thou shalt forget the shame of thy youth, and shalt not remember the reproach of thy widowhood any more. [5]For thy Maker is thine husband; the LORD of hosts is his name; and thy Redeemer the Holy One of Israel; The God of the whole earth shall he be called.

Here is a woman that is barren, with no children and apparently incapable of having any. This is a condition which was considered to be a reproach upon her family during this time period. A woman not living is desolation, shame, and sorrow. So why is God telling her to sing?

The first reason He tells her to sing is because she's blessed even before everyone else recognizes it. God declares that there are more children in her than all the women who have been having children while she was living in shame. Just because others don't see the value, doesn't mean that it's not there!

1 John 3:2 (KJV) ²Beloved, now are we the sons of God, and it doth not yet appear what we shall be: but we know that, when he shall appear, we shall be like him; for we shall see him as he is.

As children of God, there's more in us that hasn't been seen than everything the world has already displayed.

The second reason God wants us to sing, even before our territory produces its fruit is because it keeps the principalities out and thus keeps out the territorial drama.

Singing is simply a form of praise that means to rejoice; to "halal", "barak", "yadah", or "shaback" God in song. It invites God into our territory!

Psalm 22:3 (KJV) ³But thou art holy, O thou that inhabitest the praises of Israel.

The enemy can't stay in the same place where God is dwelling and neither can his territorial drama. Every time we praise God, He enters into that praise; and when He enters, the drama leaves. It not only leaves, it is blocked from getting back in!

Psalm 34:1 (KJV) ¹I will bless the LORD at all times: his praise shall continually be in my mouth.

Psalm 34:7 (KJV) ⁷The angel of the LORD encampeth round about them that fear him, and delivereth them.

When we praise God, He dispatches angels around our territory to protect us from invaders.

Stand Up To The Intimidators

Isaiah 54:2-3 (KJV) ²Enlarge the place of thy tent, and let them stretch forth the curtains of thine habitations: spare not, lengthen thy cords, and strengthen thy stakes; ³For thou shalt break forth on the right hand and on the left; and thy seed shall inherit the Gentiles, and make the desolate cities to be inhabited.

God calls us to enlarge, stretch forth, lengthen, and strengthen! Why? Because we are about to break forth on the right and the left; that is we will be busting at the seams. What we have is not big enough to hold what we're going to have. So God says expand! We need to expand our territory, our relationships, our businesses, our friendships, and our ministries, because we can't hold what is coming.

Malachi 3:10 (KJV) [10]Bring ye all the tithes into the storehouse, that there may be meat in mine house, and prove me now herewith, saith the LORD of hosts, if I will not open you the windows of heaven, and pour you out a blessing, that there shall not be room enough to receive it.

When you expand into new territory, there will be intimidators with territorial drama to run you out and keep you out.

Matthew 11:12 (KJV) [12]And from the days of John the Baptist until now the kingdom of heaven suffereth violence, and the violent take it by force.

If you are going to advance, you are going to have to stand up to the intimidators! This means standing your ground without fear.

Isaiah 54:4 (KJV) [4]Fear not; for thou shalt not be ashamed: neither be thou confounded; for thou shalt not be put to shame: for thou shalt forget the shame of thy youth, and shalt not remember the reproach of thy widowhood any more.

An intimidator is nothing but a bully and the power of a bully is derived from the fear of those he or she is trying to intimidate. God does not want us operating out of fear because He has not given us the spirit of fear. Neither does He want us fighting their evil drama with more evil drama because He told us to avenge not ourselves, but to overcome evil with good. So how do we do this? We simply stand up to the bullies, the intimidators, and the territorial spirits by standing on the Word of God.

Matthew 24:35 (KJV) ³⁵*Heaven and earth shall pass away, but my words shall not pass away.*

Stand Up With God's Word

Isaiah 54:15-16 (KJV) ¹⁵*Behold, they shall surely gather together, but not by me: whosoever shall gather together against thee shall fall for thy sake.* ¹⁶*Behold, I have created the smith that bloweth the coals in the fire, and that bringeth forth an instrument for his work; and I have created the waster to destroy.*

God says they will surely come; our enemies will surely plot against us trying to destroy us. They will gather in numbers to overwhelm you, but He wants us to stand on the promises of His Word.

His Word tells us not to worry about the territorial spirits that come to invade and destroy us, because first and foremost because He created them. God created the blacksmith (the maker of the weapons), and the waster or army (the users of the weapons); and since He created them, He knows everything about them. As a matter of fact, He knows more about them than they know about themselves and that same God is our Father and He will not allow more on us than we can bear.

1 Corinthians 10:13 (KJV) [13]There hath no temptation taken you but such as is common to man: but God is faithful, who will not suffer you to be tempted above that ye are able; but will with the temptation also make a way to escape, that ye may be able to bear it.

God created the people who lie on us, who betray us and those who plot against us, but He will not allow their lies, betrayal, or plots to destroy us. So, we can stand up knowing that none of these weapons will work against us.

Isaiah 54:17 (KJV) [17]No weapon that is formed against thee shall prosper; and every tongue that shall rise against thee in judgment thou shalt condemn. This is the heritage of the servants of the LORD, and their righteousness is of me, saith the LORD.

Lead Us Not (Temptation Drama)

One of the biggest problems with relationships is that they seldom end up where they were headed when they started. A marriage starts out with a vow of "till death do us part", headed for a lifetime of love, companionship, and partnership, but instead ends in divorce. Two people start out as best friends, or "BFF's" (Best Friends Forever), but instead end up not talking to each other. A young man starts working at a new company intending to have a long career with them, but instead quits after a year disappointed at the lack of progress. A family joins a church with plans to work in ministry, but instead leave after a few years frustrated with members and/or the pastor.

In life we start out on a path with a destination in mind, but many times we end up at a destination totally opposite to where we were headed. Perhaps you have started out in a normal conversation that ended up in a heated argument. Or maybe you have found yourself in a compromising situation, that you swore to yourself you would never allow. Then there is the quest for the fulfillment of a certain desire to the point where you feel like you will die if you don't get it. But once you get it you almost wish you were dead!

Jeremiah 29:11 (KJV) *[11] For I know the thoughts that I think toward you, saith the LORD, thoughts of peace, and not of evil, to give you an expected end.*

So how do we end up so far off from where we intended to go? How do we end up with things or in situations that we thought we needed, but now wish we never had? The answer to these questions is the temptations that lead us astray. These temptations are produced by the Rulers of the Darkness of this World.

Ephesians 6:12 (KJV) [12]For we wrestle not against flesh and blood, but against principalities, against powers, against the rulers of the darkness of this world, against spiritual wickedness in high places.

The Rulers of the Darkness create situations of drama that wreak havoc in our relationships by tempting our flesh to go after something God doesn't want us to have; by tempting our eyes to see something that God is not showing us; and by tempting us to think of ourselves more highly than we ought. Ultimately, these temptations lead us down a path away from our purpose, calling, blessings, and destiny.

1 John 2: 16 (KJV) [16]For all that is in the world, the lust of the flesh, and the lust of the eyes, and the pride of life, is not of the Father, but is of the world.

When Jesus taught us to pray, one of the things He taught us to pray for on a daily basis was to not be lead into or by temptations.

Matthew 6:13 (KJV) [13]*And lead us not into temptation, but deliver us from evil: For thine is the kingdom, and the power, and the glory, forever. Amen.*

Don't Be Led By Your Flesh (Path of Regret)

Deliverance from the drama of temptations requires several things. The first is to not be led by our flesh.

Galatians 5:17 (KJV) [17]*For the flesh lusteth against the Spirit, and the Spirit against the flesh: and these are contrary the one to the other: so that ye cannot do the things that ye would.*

The drama of the flesh always leads us down a path of regret. A fight we wish we wouldn't have had; an action we wish we wouldn't have taken; a move we wish we wouldn't have made; a word we wish we wouldn't have said. What is even worse about being led down this path of regret is the fact that we are led down this path over and over!

The reason for this continual downward spiral is the combination of the lusts of our flesh and the temptations of the Rulers of the Darkness of This World!

Romans 7:18 (KJV) [18]*For I know that in me (that is, in my flesh,) dwelleth no good thing: for to will is present with me; but how to perform that which is good I find not.*

Romans 7:21 (KJV) ^{21}I find then a law, that, when I would do good, evil is present with me.

James 1:14-15 (KJV) ^{14}But every man is tempted, when he is drawn away of his own lust, and enticed. ^{15}Then when lust hath conceived, it bringeth forth sin: and sin, when it is finished, bringeth forth death.

The Rulers of the Darkness of This World use the temptations in the world to lure us by the lusts of our flesh. They lead us away from God's plan for our lives. Although we don't want to go down this path, our flesh craves it. Our flesh wants to constantly be fed. Unfortunately, the consequence of feeding our flesh is destruction.

Romans 7:19-20 (KJV) ^{19}For the good that I would I do not: but the evil which I would not, that I do. ^{20}Now if I do that I would not, it is no more I that do it, but sin that dwelleth in me.

Romans 7:24 (KJV) ^{24}O wretched man that I am! who shall deliver me from the body of this death?

The answer to who shall deliver us from this predicament is to change what we feed it: the flesh or the spirit.

Galatians 5:16-17 (KJV) [16]This I say then, Walk in the Spirit, and ye shall not fulfil the lust of the flesh. [17]For the flesh lusteth against the Spirit, and the Spirit against the flesh: and these are contrary the one to the other: so that ye cannot do the things that ye would.

To walk in the spirit means to feed the Holy Spirit in us. To fulfill the lust of the flesh means to feed the flesh, that is us, and according to the bible, we can't do both. We feed the spirit and starve the flesh; or we feed the flesh and starve the spirit.

Luke 16:13 (KJV) [13]No servant can serve two masters: for either he will hate the one, and love the other; or else he will hold to the one, and despise the other. Ye cannot serve God and mammon.

If we don't want to be led by our flesh we have to choose to starve it by feeding the spirit. The first Psalm teaches us how to do this.

Psalm 1:1-2 (KJV) [1]Blessed is the man that walketh not in the counsel of the ungodly, nor standeth in the way of sinners, nor sitteth in the seat of the scornful. [2]But his delight is in the law of the LORD; and in his law doth he meditate day and night.

The scripture is basically telling us to change the company that we keep. We are not to follow the advice of the wicked, hang around with sinners, or join in with those that complain or ridicule the things of God. This type of company produces evil communications and evil communications will corrupt us and drive us to feed our flesh.

1 Corinthians 15:33 (KJV) ³³Be not deceived: evil communications corrupt good manners.

However, when we meditate on the Word of God, the communication that fills us is His Word, His promises, and His blessings.

Psalm 1:2-3 (KJV) ²But his delight is in the law of the LORD; and in his law doth he meditate day and night. ³And he shall be like a tree planted by the rivers of water, that bringeth forth his fruit in his season; his leaf also shall not wither; and whatsoever he doeth shall prosper.

Don't Be Led By Your Eyes (Path of Fear)

The second thing that the deliverance from the drama of temptations requires is not to be lead by our eyes.

There's an old saying that goes, "look before you leap"; but for some of us, looking is what got us into trouble in the first place. The problem with our eyes is that the enemy can show us things that are antithetical to God's plan, causing us to make a move out of His will.

The drama comes about when we see something in people, or they see something in us that activates our flesh. The eyes are the window to the soul (mind, will, emotions); and what we see impacts our soul causing us to make emotional decisions, choices, and actions. Many times these emotional actions will be out of the will of God and the plan He has for our lives.

The key to dealing with the lust of the eyes, and not be driven by the emotions that stimulated in us; is to stop looking, and start watching.

1 Thessalonians 5:6 (KJV) ⁶Therefore let us not sleep, as do others; but let us watch and be sober.

The word *sober* comes from the Greek word nēphō, which is to keep sober, to be calm and collected in spirit; to watch.

To *look* is to use the natural senses of your eyes, but to *watch* is to use the spiritual senses of your faith. We need to stop looking at what the enemy is showing us, and start watching what the Spirit is revealing to us.

Luke 21:36 (KJV) ³⁶Watch ye therefore, and pray always, that ye may be accounted worthy to

escape all these things that shall come to pass, and to
stand before the Son of man.

*1 Peter 4:7 (KJV) [7]But the end of all things is at
hand: be ye therefore sober, and watch unto prayer.*

Prayer is not a one way lecture to God about what we want, but a two way conversation to hear what He's saying to us. That two way conversation is about coming to God through faith.

*Hebrews 11:6 (KJV) [6]But without faith it is
impossible to please him: for he that cometh to God
must believe that he is, and that he is a rewarder of
them that diligently seek him.*

As Christians we are taught to walk by faith (watch) and not by sight. The Bible teaches us that faith comes by hearing, and hearing by the word of God. If we watch through our faith; then we don't use our eyes, we use our ears.

*Revelation 2:7 (KJV) [7]He that hath an ear, let
him hear what the Spirit saith unto the churches; To
him that overcometh will I give to eat of the tree of
life, which is in the midst of the paradise of God.*

Don't Be Led By Yourself (Path of Pride / Arrogance)

Jesus told us to pray, "Lead us not into temptations, but deliver us from evil." That prayer gives us the solution to dealing with the temptations of this world; don't let them lead us. First, we must not be led by our flesh. We do this by feeding our spirit and starving our flesh. Second, we must not be led by our eyes. We do this by watching with our faith and blinding our eyes. Lastly, we must not be led by our self. We do this by humbling ourselves.

1 John 2:16 (KJV) *[16]For all that is in the world, the lust of the flesh, and the lust of the eyes, and the pride of life, is not of the Father, but is of the world.*

Our human nature is to be lifted up as a result of self; led by self preservation which is a form of pride. The reason why self preservation is pride, is because the most important thing to us is our own self, life, emotions, and feelings. It is natural for us to protect ourselves.

The pride of life is not simply about being arrogant, but developing a lifestyle that protects one's self, feelings, or emotions. This is contrary to what God requires of us.

Luke 9:23 (KJV) *[23]And he said to them all, If any man will come after me, let him deny himself, and take up his cross daily, and follow me.*

Deliverance from the pride of life requires us to deny our self, feelings and emotions and to follow Christ.

James 4:6 (KJV) ⁶But he giveth more grace. Wherefore he saith, God resisteth the proud, but giveth grace unto the humble.

Matthew 23:12 (KJV) ¹²And whosoever shall exalt himself shall be abased; and he that shall humble himself shall be exalted.

Philippians 2:8-11 (KJV) ⁸And being found in fashion as a man, he humbled himself, and became obedient unto death, even the death of the cross. ⁹Wherefore God also hath highly exalted him, and given him a name which is above every name: ¹⁰That at the name of Jesus every knee should bow, of things in heaven, and things in earth, and things under the earth; ¹¹And that every tongue should confess that Jesus Christ is Lord, to the glory of God the Father.

Matthew 5:5 (KJV) ⁵Blessed are the meek: for they shall inherit the earth.

When we humble ourselves, we are being led by the Spirit of God. Our humility allows God to exalt us, bless us, and give us everything He's destined for us that glorifies Him.

Help Is On The Way (Spiritual Drama)

The last form of drama that we deal with is Spiritual Wickedness in High Places, which represents the unclean spirits who have charge over religion. They operate in the realm of religion, church, and spirituality to create havoc in the very place where people come to receive help. This drama comes in the form of church hurt, spiritual abuse, and delays and setbacks at a spiritual level.

Ephesians 6:12 (KJV) [12]For we wrestle not against flesh and blood, but against principalities, against powers, against the rulers of the darkness of this world, against spiritual wickedness in high places.

Church hurt and spiritual abuse are perhaps the most reprehensible forms of attack on an individual. It's reprehensible because it is a kin to kicking a person while they are down. When people come to church it is an acknowledgement that they can't do it by themselves, and that it's going to take God to do it for them. These forces cause church hurt that lead people to give up on the church; spiritual abuse that lead people to give up on church leaders; and delays and setbacks that lead people to give up on God.

It's like giving up on the entire medical profession because of being treated at a poor hospital, seen by a bad doctor, or being given the wrong medicine that didn't work.

Just because we were hurt in the church, abused by church leaders, or haven't seen our blessing yet; doesn't mean that God has not heard our cry.

When the place of our help becomes the source of our hurt; when our helper becomes our abuser; the enemy wants us to believe that it's hopeless. Since they can't stop our blessings or our help; they withstand and delay it. Daniel had such an experience.

Daniel 10:12-14 (KJV) *[12]Then said he unto me, Fear not, Daniel: for from the first day that thou didst set thine heart to understand, and to chasten thyself before thy God, thy words were heard, and I am come for thy words. [13]But the prince of the kingdom of Persia withstood me one and twenty days: but, lo, Michael, one of the chief princes, came to help me; and I remained there with the kings of Persia. [14]Now I am come to make thee understand what shall befall thy people in the latter days: for yet the vision is for many days.*

Whether it's been three weeks, three months, or three years, we must always remember that delay does not necessarily mean denied. We must never give up hope even when we experience hurt because help is always on the way.

Spiritual Drama From Hurt And Abuse

Church hurt is really no different than any other form of hurt we experience. It just becomes exacerbated, made worse or intensified because of where it happened; in the church.

The reality is hurt is hurt, betrayal is betrayal, disappointment is disappointment. But there is something about the human psyche that makes it appear to be worse when it comes from within the church. People have been hurt and disappointed all their lives, but when it comes from those they put their trust in, those they thought would help them, it becomes even more hurtful.

She was my sister in the Lord, He's supposed to be a minister, How could they do that? I go to church with them; are all things we have either said or heard from people who have been hurt in the church.

Then there is spiritual abuse! This is when the hurt comes from someone who is in authority in the church; a pastor or church leader, who abuses that authority to take advantage of those who have given him or her that authority over them.

So, what do you do when the place you went to for help, turns out to give you hurt instead? What do you do when those you trusted in abuse that trust?

Well we know what the enemy wants us to do. He wants us to leave. But if we leave, we are leaving our help.

Psalm 46:1-3 (KJV) [1]God is our refuge and strength, a very present help in trouble. [2]Therefore will not we fear, though the earth be removed, and though the mountains be carried into the midst of the sea; [3]Though the waters thereof roar and be troubled, though the mountains shake with the swelling thereof. Selah.

What we have to do is recognize the type of spiritual abuse we are dealing with. Is it hurt and abuse that is intentional or is it out of ignorance? Some people hurt us because they are simply spiritually immature or ignorant of the harm they are causing. However, there are those who know exactly what they are doing, and are doing it intentionally. Let's look at these intentional spiritual abusers.

2 Timothy 3:1-7 (KJV) [1]This know also, that in the last days perilous times shall come. [2]For men shall be lovers of their own selves, covetous, boasters, proud, blasphemers, disobedient to parents, unthankful, unholy, [3]Without natural affection, trucebreakers, false accusers, incontinent, fierce, despisers of those that are good, [4]Traitors, heady, highminded, lovers of pleasures more than lovers of God; [5]Having a form of godliness, but denying the power thereof: from such turn away. [6]For of this sort are they which creep into houses, and lead captive silly women laden with sins, led away with divers lusts, ⁷Ever learning, and never able to come to the knowledge of the truth.

The key verse here is verse five which says that these wicked people are in the church "Having a form of godliness, but denying the power thereof; from such turn away." The new living translation quotes this verse as follows, "They will act as if they are religious, but they will reject the power that could make them godly. You must stay away from people like that." The way we deal with these wicked church people is to turn away and stay away from them; and turn to the Word of God.

John 8:31-32 (NLT) ³¹Jesus said to the people who believed in him, "You are truly my disciples if you keep obeying my teachings. ³²And you will know the truth, and the truth will set you free."

Turn to the Word for freedom. Get out from under the bondage of these people, refuse to be their victims and embrace the freedom that Christ brings.

Galatians 5:1 (KJV) ¹Stand fast therefore in the liberty wherewith Christ hath made us free, and be not entangled again with the yoke of bondage.

2 Corinthians 3:17 (KJV) *[17]Now the Lord is that Spirit: and where the Spirit of the Lord is, there is liberty.*

Now, what do we do about those people in the church that hurt us out of ignorance because of their spiritual immaturity? We are hurt nevertheless, but intent is a mitigating factor. Jesus responded to His disciples in a situation that could be interpreted as hurt coming from spiritually immature Christians in the 17th chapter of Luke.

Luke 17:1-5 (KJV) *[1]Then said he unto the disciples, It is impossible but that offences will come: but woe unto him, through whom they come! [2]It were better for him that a millstone were hanged about his neck, and he cast into the sea, than that he should offend one of these little ones. [3]Take heed to yourselves: If thy brother trespass against thee, rebuke him; and if he repent, forgive him. [4]And if he trespass against thee seven times in a day, and seven times in a day turn again to thee, saying, I repent; thou shalt forgive him. [5]And the apostles said unto the Lord, Increase our faith.*

What is really interesting here is what we see in the last two verses. In verse 4, Jesus says if they wrong you seven times in one day, you must forgive them seven times. But in verse 5 the disciples are frank and honest and say, Lord we are not there yet; we need your help to increase our faith.

We do not have the capacity to forgive and forget like God does, which is why it is probably just as difficult for us to forgive a person seven times in one day. Instead of allowing their ignorance or immaturity to destroy us, Jesus says increase your faith. We have to let them go, and go after God by increasing our faith.

Hebrews 11:6 (KJV) ⁶But without faith it is impossible to please him: for he that cometh to God must believe that he is, and that he is a rewarder of them that diligently seek him.

Romans 10:17 (KJV) ¹⁷So then faith cometh by hearing, and hearing by the word of God.

Spiritual Drama from Delays and Setbacks

We all have experienced delays and setbacks in our lives, but perhaps have not thought of them in terms of Spiritual Wickedness in High Places. This is what Daniel experienced for three weeks as the answer to his prayers were delayed.

Daniel 10:2 (KJV) ²In those days I Daniel was mourning three full weeks.

For three weeks Daniel prayed, fasted, and wept before the Lord, but received no answer. Perhaps just like many of us; waiting for an answer, a blessing, a breakthrough, or simply just a word that seems like it will never get here.

We pray but hear nothing; we give but receive nothing; we praise but have nothing; we believe but see nothing; we lose but find nothing.

The delays are bad enough; a promotion that should have come three years ago is still not here; a house that you've been trying to get for five years, but are still paying rent. Add to the frustration of the delay, the struggle of the setback. For example, you already don't have enough money to make ends meet from a job that you should have gotten a raise from last year and you get laid off.

Then there is the spiritual drama that comes to frustrate us as we see wicked people getting ahead.

Psalm 73:1-3 (KJV) [1]Truly God is good to Israel, even to such as are of a clean heart. [2]But as for me, my feet were almost gone; my steps had well nigh slipped. [3]For I was envious at the foolish, when I saw the prosperity of the wicked.

We must understand why the enemy uses delays or setbacks. He uses setbacks and delays to get us to give up on our blessings so that we deny the source of them. In the book of Job, Job's wife got to this place when she told him to curse God and die. This is exactly what the enemy is trying to get us to do.

The 121st Psalm teaches us that regardless of the delay, the setback, the hurt, or even the abuse, we are to keep looking to our source of help because help is on the way.

We must keep looking, fret not, and hold on!

Psalm 121:1-3 (KJV) [1]I will lift up mine eyes unto the hills, from whence cometh my help. [2]My help cometh from the LORD, which made heaven and earth. [3]He will not suffer thy foot to be moved: he that keepeth thee will not slumber.

The enemy wants to depress us by showing us what the wicked is doing, but God says fret not, stop worrying about the wicked for they shall soon wither and fade away.

Psalm 37:1-2 (KJV) [1]Fret not thyself because of evildoers, neither be thou envious against the workers of iniquity. [2]For they shall soon be cut down like the grass, and wither as the green herb.

Lastly, God wants us to hold on because help is on the way. Job who was at the point where he wanted to die as a result of spiritual wickedness by Satan decides that he cannot die because he had to be there when his season changed. He said to himself, I've got to hold on!

Job 14:14 (KJV) [14]If a man die, shall he live again? all the days of my appointed time will I wait, till my change come.

Galatians 6:9 (KJV) [9]And let us not be weary in well doing: for in due season we shall reap, if we faint not.

Spiritual Victory From Spiritual Reinforcements

Perhaps one of the most powerful reasons we should hold on is because we have spiritual reinforcement.

Daniel 10:12 (NLT) [12]Then he said, "Don't be afraid, Daniel. Since the first day you began to pray for understanding and to humble yourself before your God, your request has been heard in heaven. I have come in answer to your prayer.

Daniel's answer was delayed but it wasn't denied. Not only was it not denied, it was answered from the very moment he set his heart to ask. We must understand that even before we can get the request out of our mouth, God has already answered and we can praise God when the answer is delayed, because we have spiritual reinforcement to back up what God said.

Isaiah 65:24 (NLT) [24]I will answer them before they even call to me. While they are still talking to me about their needs, I will go ahead and answer their prayers!

Daniel 10:13 (NLT) [13]But for twenty-one days the spirit prince of the kingdom of Persia blocked my way. Then Michael, one of the archangels, came to help me, and I left him there with the spirit prince of the kingdom of Persia.

Jeremiah 29:11 (KJV) [11]For I know the thoughts that I think toward you, saith the LORD, thoughts of peace, and not of evil, to give you an expected end.

Philippians 1:6 (KJV) [6]Being confident of this very thing, that he which hath begun a good work in you will perform it until the day of Jesus Christ:

Every setback is simply another setup for more reinforcement. So when we experience setbacks, rejoice because help is on the way!

The Wickedness Of Gossip

In the previous chapters we looked at four forms of drama that devastate relationships: personal drama, territorial drama, temptation drama, and spiritual drama. Each of these forms of drama comes from the organized forces of Satan's kingdom identified in the 6th chapter of Ephesians.

Ephesians 6:12 (KJV) [12]For we wrestle not against flesh and blood, but against principalities, against powers, against the rulers of the darkness of this world, against spiritual wickedness in high places.

Gossip, however is found in each of these four areas of drama, and is extremely wicked because it appears to be innocent as it touches nearly everyone. The ultimate gossiper was Satan.

Revelation 12:9-11 (KJV) [9]And the great dragon was cast out, that old serpent, called the Devil, and Satan, which deceiveth the whole world: he was cast out into the earth, and his angels were cast out with him. [10]And I heard a loud voice saying in heaven, Now is come salvation, and strength, and the kingdom of our God, and the power of his Christ: for the accuser of our brethren is cast down, which accused them before our God day and night. [11]And they overcame him by the blood of the Lamb, and by the word of their testimony; and they loved not their lives unto the death.

God absolutely hates gossip. He hates it so much that He calls it an abomination.

Proverbs 6:16-19 (KJV) [16]These six things doth the LORD hate: yea, seven are an abomination unto him: [17]A proud look, a lying tongue, and hands that shed innocent blood, [18]An heart that deviseth wicked imaginations, feet that be swift in running to mischief, [19]A false witness that speaketh lies, and he that soweth discord among brethren.

What makes gossip so bad is the fact that once it is deployed, it cannot be retracted. The following story depicts why gossip is so devastating:

A woman had gossiped about a man and when she realized what she had done, went to him and apologized. She said she would do anything to make up for the cruel things she had said. He told her to take a sack full of feathers and to go to a certain street corner and cast the feathers to the wind. She did and when she had finished came back and reported. The gentleman then directed her to go back and retrieve every feather. She exclaimed that is impossible, the wind has scattered them everywhere. So it is with the things you have said, he replied, there is no way to repair the damage that you have done.

Gossip is one of those devices that the enemy uses to destroy us and destroy our relationships with each other. It breaks up families and friendships, destroys marriages and workplace relationships, and even breaks up spiritual families by driving people away from the church. It even causes our children to grow up with dysfunctional views on relationships driving them away from family, church, and even the Lord. Imagine what goes through the mind of a child when they constantly see their parents smiling in the faces of brothers and sisters at church and then talking about them on the ride home from church.

Gossip has probably done more harm to relationships than anything else. Is there any wonder why God hates it and calls it an abomination! If God hates it, then we need to hate it. If it's an abomination in the sight of God, it needs to be in ours. The problem is not the person being gossiped about; it is the person doing the gossiping.

So why do people gossip? Some gossip because they are carnally minded (not spiritual); and the reason why people listen to gossip is for the same reason. A carnally minded person is concerned about self, whereas a spiritually minded person is concerned for others.

1 Corinthians 3:3 (KJV) ³For ye are yet carnal: for whereas there is among you envying, and strife, and divisions, are ye not carnal, and walk as men?

Others gossip because in reality they hate the person they are gossiping about. They may not have stated it, but their hate has driven them to tear down the other person.

Proverbs 10:18 (KJV) *[18]He that hideth hatred with lying lips, and he that uttereth a slander, is a fool.*

The last reason people gossip is because they are idle. These are people who do not have a life and want to feel important, so they gossip.

1 Timothy 5:13 (KJV) *[13]And withal they learn to be idle, wandering about from house to house; and not only idle, but tattlers also and busybodies, speaking things which they ought not.*

Notice that those who gossip aren't doing anything spiritually; and the ones they are gossiping about are those who are doing the work of the Lord.

The reason why gossip is so pervasive is because of the lack of love!

1 Corinthians 13:4-5 (NLT) *[4]Love is patient and kind. Love is not jealous or boastful or proud [5]or rude. Love does not demand its own way. Love is not irritable, and it keeps no record of when it has been wronged.*

Simply put, God's love makes it impossible for Christians to hate one another. So then the strife, conflict, and discord can only be built up because of a lack of love. Since we are Christians, it must be done in secret!

Psalm 101:5 (NLT) *[5]I will not tolerate people who slander their neighbors. I will not endure conceit and pride.*

True Christian love, called agape love, would eradicate gossip, because it would destroy the discord and conflict before it could get started. Every relationship needs someone to have Godly Love (Agape). This would produce covenant relationships that are immune to gossip, as opposed to the contractual relationships that are burdened and susceptible to gossip. We must learn how to deal with our reality, and it is gossip.

There are always three parties to gossip:

1. The Perpetrator: this is the architect, executor, doer of the gossip! The person that is responsible for or behind the gossip.
2. The Enabler: the facilitator that allows or permits; the person that makes gossip possible.
3. The Victim: the injured party; the one that is wounded or suffers from gossip.

The answer for the perpetrator, the enabler, and the victim of gossip is to become free from the bondage of this wicked device.

2 Corinthians 3:17 (NLT) ^{17}*Now, the Lord is the Spirit, and wherever the Spirit of the Lord is, he gives freedom.*

John 8:32 (NLT) ^{32}*And you will know the truth, and the truth will set you free."*

Freedom will not come from chasing down the lies, or from confronting betrayers; it will only come from the power of God's Spirit and the truth of His Word.

Overcoming The Perpetrator

There are two types of perpetrators when it comes to gossip. There's the lying gossiper and the betraying gossiper. The goal of every Christian is to overcome both types of gossipers.

To overcome the lying gossiper we must learn how to deal with anger. When a person lies on you, it produces the emotion of anger. That anger, if left unchecked, will produce the behavior of vengeance. The Bible teaches us to be angry and sin not and that sin is the sin of vengeance, that is produced from lying.

Ephesians 4:25-27 (KJV) [25]Wherefore putting away lying, speak every man truth with his neighbour: for we are members one of another. [26]Be ye angry, and sin not: let not the sun go down upon your wrath: [27]Neither give place to the devil.

The Bible says be angry, but sin not. We have to overcome the emotion of anger so that we can deny the action of vengeance!

Romans 12:19 (KJV) [19]Dearly beloved, avenge not yourselves, but rather give place unto wrath: for it is written, Vengeance is mine; I will repay, saith the Lord.

When a person lies on you it's like being hit without provocation and taking it is one of the hardest things to do!

It is like the Irishman who was hit on one cheek, and he got up and turned the other cheek. This time the fellow hit him so hard, he knocked him down. Then the Irishman got up and beat the stuffings out of the other fellow. Someone asked him, "Why in the world did you do that? You turned the other cheek; why didn't you leave it like that?" "Well," he said, "the Bible says to turn your cheek, and I had only one other cheek to turn. The Lord didn't tell me what to do after that, so I did what I thought I ought to do."

This is what most of us do. We find it difficult not to hit back. The minute we take the matter into our own hands and attempt to work it out by hitting back as hard as we can, we have taken the matter out of God's control, and we are no longer walking by faith.

The key to overcoming perpetrators of gossip is to first keep the faith that God will take care of it and us; because we walk by faith and not by sight. Secondly, we must do the opposite of what is expected.

Romans 12:20 (KJV) [20]*Therefore if thine enemy hunger, feed him; if he thirst, give him drink: for in so doing thou shalt heap coals of fire on his head.*

The lying gossiper expects us to act out of vengeance, but instead we need to act out of love.

On the other hand, to overcome the betraying gossiper, we must learn to deal with hurt. Unlike a lie that produces anger, betrayal produces hurt and hurt causes depression, which in turn produces inaction.

A person excited by their new relationship in the church, but becomes a victim of church hurt, could decide they don't want to do anything in the church and subsequently lose their motivation, quit, and just give up. The only way to get over hurt is to deny your flesh and in turn deny the natural response to the pain of that hurt.

When a person is hurt, the natural response is to withdraw from the thing that is causing the hurt, which makes sense from a natural perspective. From a spiritual perspective it is exactly the opposite of what we should do.

Luke 9:23 (KJV) [23] And he said to them all, If any man will come after me, let him deny himself, and take up his cross daily, and follow me.

Don't run from the cross, embrace the cross and wear it as a badge of honor. As Christians, we are supposed to take up our cross of pain. There will be many afflictions and our responsibility is not to run from them, but have joy when they come; because we know that there is a bigger purpose behind the pain.

Psalm 34:19 (KJV) [19] Many are the afflictions of the righteous: but the LORD delivereth him out of them all.

James 1:2-3 (KJV) [2] My brethren, count it all joy when ye fall into divers temptations; [3] Knowing this, that the trying of your faith worketh patience.

They expected us to go down and stay down, but instead we get up and stay up; instead of crying, we rejoiced.

Overcoming The Enabler

One of the things we must understand when it comes to gossip is that it is like fire, it can only work as long as you have a fuel source. Gossip only works when it has people who are willing to be the wood, the source of fuel to keep it going.

Proverbs 26:20 (KJV) [20] Where no wood is, there the fire goeth out: so where there is no talebearer, the strife ceaseth.

The main issue with enablers is they have heard some lie about us; and since we know that it's easier to believe a lie than to accept the truth, we get concerned with how many people believe the lie. We must understand this is not our problem, it is theirs! We know the truth and the Bible says that the truth shall make us free. They are the ones in bondage with the lie! Not only do we know the truth, but God knows the truth. We need to stop being worried about what other people think about us when we know that it is a lie and rejoice at what God thinks about us.

Jeremiah 29:11 (KJV) [11] For I know the thoughts that I think toward you, saith the LORD, thoughts of peace, and not of evil, to give you an expected end.

We have to be careful with people whose only conversation is to tell us something negative about others and say "it's a secret." First, if they will tell you something about another person, then they will tell another person something about you. When people say, "I've got to tell you something, but you can't tell anyone", the truth is they really want you to tell it. If they truly wanted to keep it a secret, they wouldn't have told you in the first place.

Psalm 101:5 (KJV) [5]Whoso privily slandereth his neighbour, him will I cut off: him that hath an high look and a proud heart will not I suffer.

To "privly slander" means to gossip in secret; and God's response to those that gossip in secret is to cut them off. We must refuse to be their wood.

Proverbs 11:13 (KJV) [13]A talebearer revealeth secrets: but he that is of a faithful spirit concealeth the matter.

A gossiper takes malicious delight in spreading scandal, telling on others, and breaking confidences. They don't hold anything back, but tell everything they know. Their goal is to get it out to as many people as possible. A faithful friend maintains a confidence and refrains from talking.

Since God says He will cut them off, we need to cut them off. The first way we cut them off is by unveiling the cloak of secrecy.

1 Timothy 5:19 (KJV) [19] *Against an elder receive not an accusation, but before two or three witnesses.*

We cut them off by demanding witnesses. They want to throw the rocks and hide their hands, but when you demand witnesses, they lose the veil of secrecy. If a person can't say it in front of their face, then they shouldn't say it behind their back.

Lastly, we must refuse to allow them to feed our spirit with negativity.

Luke 6:45 (KJV) [45] *A good man out of the good treasure of his heart bringeth forth that which is good; and an evil man out of the evil treasure of his heart bringeth forth that which is evil: for of the abundance of the heart his mouth speaketh.*

When people keep bringing you negative gossip, it is because negativity is in their heart. If you are not careful, that same negativity will fill yours. If we continually allow people to feed us negativity, it will get in our heart. If it gets in our heart, then we will speak it. If we speak it, we will become it.

Proverbs 18:21 (KJV) [21] *Death and life are in the power of the tongue: and they that love it shall eat the fruit thereof.*

When you want life, you can't allow people to continue speaking death to you. When you want joy, you can't allow people to speak sorrow and depression. Instead, you need a steady diet of uplifting thoughts.

Philippians 4:8 (KJV) [8]Finally, brethren, whatsoever things are true, whatsoever things are honest, whatsoever things are just, whatsoever things are pure, whatsoever things are lovely, whatsoever things are of good report; if there be any virtue, and if there be any praise, think on these things.

Overcome Because You Are An Over Comer!

Revelation 12:10-11 (KJV) [10]And I heard a loud voice saying in heaven, Now is come salvation, and strength, and the kingdom of our God, and the power of his Christ: for the accuser of our brethren is cast down, which accused them before our God day and night. [11]And they overcame him by the blood of the Lamb, and by the word of their testimony; and they loved not their lives unto the death.

To be an over comer of gossip, we must refuse to be a victim of it. We must refuse to be a victim of the perpetrators of gossip. What they do is tell lies and we know the truth. We must refuse to be a victim of the enablers. If they believe the lie, then that is their problem and not ours. We know what God thinks and has already said about us.

Romans 8:37 (KJV) *³⁷Nay, in all these things we are more than conquerors through him that loved us.*

They are going to accuse us day and night; they are going to gossip and tell lies; they are going to break our confidence; but since we are more than conquerors, we will overcome.

We don't have to worry because Christ worried; we don't have to fight because Christ fought; we don't have to die because Christ died; we simply need to overcome.

PART 2: Developing An Immunity To Drama

Established In The Midst Of Drama

When most people think about the phrase "No More Drama", they think of it in terms of finding a place, location, business, relationship, or church where there is no drama. They set out to find this mystical place or these mystical people who have no drama, but ultimately they fail!

Luke 17:1 It is impossible but that offences will come: but woe unto him through whom they come!

Psalm 34:19 Many are the afflictions of the righteous: but the Lord delivereth him out of them all.

Matthew 11:12 (KJV) 12And from the days of John the Baptist until now the kingdom of heaven suffereth violence, and the violent take it by force.

They fail to find this place or these people because it (or them) does not exist. People are not perfect so they will fail us and commit offences against us. We are Christians and will be attacked if for no other reason than we belong to God and because our calling to expand the Kingdom of Heaven is about war against Satan's kingdom.

"No More Drama" is about a lifestyle in which we live, in a world full of drama, but refuse to allow the world and its drama to infiltrate us. A "Drama Free

Lifestyle" is about being established in a world full of drama with immunity to drama so that we are not pulled down by it. Since we have immunity, we are able to help those who cannot help themselves by becoming the light of the world that Christ chose us to become.

Matthew 5:13-14 (KJV) ¹³*Ye are the salt of the earth: but if the salt have lost his savour, wherewith shall it be salted? it is thenceforth good for nothing, but to be cast out, and to be trodden under foot of men.* ¹⁴*Ye are the light of the world. A city that is set on an hill cannot be hid.*

Here Jesus explains why we must establish ourselves in the world. Our light brings light to the drama and our salt cures it. We establish ourselves so that we can be seen, heard, and lifted up.

Drama free marriages, careers, relationships, businesses, ministries, and churches happen not because of the world, but because of us. God calls us, anoints us, and then places and establishes us right in the middle of drama.

The immunity does not happen right away. With the power of God, we become strengthened during drama, developing a stronger anointing and more fruit of the Spirit. With this ultimately we overcome the drama of this world.

Established To Be Seen

Luke 8:26-28 (KJV) ²⁶*And they arrived at the country of the Gadarenes, which is over against Galilee.* ²⁷*And when he went forth to land, there met him out of the city a certain man, which had devils long time, and ware no clothes, neither abode in any house, but in the tombs.* ²⁸*When he saw Jesus, he cried out, and fell down before him, and with a loud voice said, what have I to do with thee, Jesus, thou Son of God most high? I beseech thee, torment me not.*

The man who was filled with drama saw Jesus and ran to Him. Although the drama fought against Jesus, ultimately the man would be delivered because Jesus was established to bring deliverance and the man saw Him.

Luke 4:18 (KJV) ¹⁸*The Spirit of the Lord is upon me, because he hath anointed me to preach the gospel to the poor; he hath sent me to heal the brokenhearted, to preach deliverance to the captives, and recovering of sight to the blind, to set at liberty them that are bruised,*

In order for us to be established and seen by the world, we must not exalt ourselves, but humble ourselves!

Matthew 23:11-12 (KJV) ¹¹*But he that is greatest among you shall be your servant.* ¹²*And whosoever shall exalt himself shall be abased; and he that shall humble himself shall be exalted.*

Matthew 5:5 (KJV) ⁵Blessed are the meek: for they shall inherit the earth.

1 Peter 5:5-7 (KJV) ⁵Likewise, ye younger, submit yourselves unto the elder. Yea, all of you be subject one to another, and be clothed with humility: for God resisteth the proud, and giveth grace to the humble. ⁶Humble yourselves therefore under the mighty hand of God, that he may exalt you in due time: ⁷Casting all your care upon him; for he careth for you.

Humility is not about being weak and submissive, hiding in a corner from people and drama, but being strong enough to stand in the middle of it without fighting back.

John 10:18 (KJV) ¹⁸No man taketh it from me, but I lay it down of myself. I have power to lay it down, and I have power to take it again. This commandment have I received of my Father.

Established To Be Heard

Once we are established to be seen, we are positioned to be heard. God makes us the light of the world in the middle of drama so that people can see the power of God in us. Once they see that power, they are ready to listen to us so that they can obtain that same power.

Acts 1:8 (KJV) *⁸But ye shall receive power, after that the Holy Ghost is come upon you: and ye shall be witnesses unto me both in Jerusalem, and in all Judaea, and in Samaria, and unto the uttermost part of the earth.*

God has called us and empowered us so that the world will listen to us. People need an answer, a solution, and we have been established to be that answer.

Established To Be Lifted Up

John 12:32 (KJV) *³²And I, if I be lifted up from the earth, will draw all men unto me.*

When Jesus said that if He be lifted up he would draw all men unto him, He was referring to being lifted up on the cross. Jesus was sent to the world as the light to be seen and He is the Word for the world to be heard. He was also the sacrifice for the world, to be its savior.

Matthew 16:24-25 (KJV) *²⁴Then said Jesus unto his disciples, If any man will come after me, let him deny himself, and take up his cross, and follow me.*

²⁵For whosoever will save his life shall lose it: and whosoever will lose his life for my sake shall find it.

When the world runs into drama, they run, fight, and do whatever is necessary from their perspective to save and protect themselves. We are called to be lifted up, to stand in humility during the drama and the personal attacks of drama. Because we are lifted up, we will draw men and women to us; that is, to the God in us who has strengthened us to stand.

The Immunity Of Identity

As we stated earlier, one need only look at the results or consequences of drama to conclude that its origins stem from the satanic activities of demons. The ruthlessness of these unclean spirits is described in the 5th chapter of Mark.

Mark 5:1-5 (KJV) [1]*And they came over unto the other side of the sea, into the country of the Gadarenes.* [2]*And when he was come out of the ship, immediately there met him out of the tombs a man with an unclean spirit,* [3]*Who had his dwelling among the tombs; and no man could bind him, no, not with chains:* [4]*Because that he had been often bound with fetters and chains, and the chains had been plucked asunder by him, and the fetters broken in pieces: neither could any man tame him.* [5]*And always, night and day, he was in the mountains, and in the tombs, crying, and cutting himself with stones.*

This uncontrollable man, living in a graveyard, on the edge of insanity, crying day and night, cutting himself with stones in an effort to alleviate the internal pain and torment of his mind was driven to this state by unclean spirits. We read later that the reason why the spirits tormented him was because they wanted to destroy his mission and purpose, which was to minister the power of Jesus Christ to the ten Greek cities of Decapolis; in essence, being the forerunner to Paul who would evangelize the Gentiles.

The disorder, devastation, pain, and torment these spirits brought to this man to prevent his mission is what they bring to all of us to prevent ours. Their goal is to operate in the early realm using spiritual means to withstand the Kingdom of God, interrupting purpose, calling, and destiny.

Ephesians 6: 12 (KJV) 12For we wrestle not against flesh and blood, but against principalities, against powers, against the rulers of the darkness of this world, against spiritual wickedness in high places.

Principalities are unclean spirits that have charge over regions and produce territorial drama. Powers are unclean spirits that are foot soldiers of personal drama on a personal level. Rulers of darkness are the forces that attack through worldly temptations. Spiritual wickedness attacks in the spiritual realm many times through religion, ministry, and churches. If we are to develop immunity to drama, we need to identify the source of the demonic force behind the drama so that we can develop the proper defense for it!

These unclean spirits bring confusion where there should be peace, hatred where there should be love, depression where there should be joy, wickedness where there should be goodness, and destruction where there should be life. Their activity manifests itself in the form of drama that causes breakups of friendships, relationships, and marriages; creates unbearable environments in the workplace leading to dismissals or people just quitting; and even produces wickedness in our churches and ministries causing church-hurt, a loss of faith, discouragement, and disillusionment.

Luke 8:26-30 (KJV) [26]And they arrived at the country of the Gadarenes, which is over against Galilee. [27]And when he went forth to land, there met him out of the city a certain man, which had devils long time, and ware no clothes, neither abode in any house, but in the tombs. [28]When he saw Jesus, he cried out, and fell down before him, and with a loud voice said, what have I to do with thee, Jesus, thou Son of God most high? I beseech thee, torment me not. [29](For he had commanded the unclean spirit to come out of the man. For oftentimes it had caught him: and he was kept bound with chains and in fetters; and he brake the bands, and was driven of the devil into the wilderness.) [30]And Jesus asked him, saying, What is thy name? And he said, Legion: because many devils were entered into him.

Drama is like a virus; a disease that comes to destroy that which is healthy. You catch it from people who are close to you, those who have direct and immediate contact with you. You cannot see it coming, but always know when you have it. Even when you recognize it early, you still know that things will get worse before they get better.

The solution to drama is just like the solution to a virus; you have to either develop immunity to it before it attacks so that it does not affect you, or strengthen your immune system so you can fight it off if you already have it.

We want to first look at developing immunity to drama. Just like a virus, the first key to developing an immunity is to identify what you are dealing with so you can develop a strategy on how to defeat it.

Ephesians 6:10-12 (KJV) 10Finally, my brethren, be strong in the Lord, and in the power of his might. 11Put on the whole armour of God, that ye may be able to stand against the wiles of the devil. 12For we wrestle not against flesh and blood, but against principalities, against powers, against the rulers of the darkness of this world, against spiritual wickedness in high places.

The Identity of Self

The "identity of self" deals with two components: who you are to yourself, and who you are to others.

Matthew 16:13-16 (KJV) ¹³When Jesus came into the coasts of Caesarea Philippi, he asked his disciples, saying, Whom do men say that I the Son of man am? ¹⁴And they said, Some say that thou art John the Baptist: some, Elias; and others, Jeremias, or one of the prophets. ¹⁵He saith unto them, But whom say ye that I am? ¹⁶And Simon Peter answered and said, Thou art the Christ, the Son of the living God.

When drama sees you, who does drama say that you are? Have you ever noticed that some people seem to always be involved, engaged in, frustrated and discombobulated over drama? Yet other people can be in the same environment, same job, or same church, and they appear to never engage in drama. It's not that drama does not exist, but it is that drama has a different reaction around certain people. Some members have said to me, "Pastor, people don't come to me with drama, because they already know that I'm going to shut it down!"

Luke 8:28-29 (KJV) 28When he saw Jesus, he cried out, and fell down before him, and with a loud voice said, What have I to do with thee, Jesus, thou Son of God most high? I beseech thee, torment me not. 29(For he had commanded the unclean spirit to come out of the man. For oftentimes it had caught him: and he was kept bound with chains and in fetters; and he brake the bands, and was driven of the devil into the wilderness.)

Up to this point, Jesus had not spoken to the drama; but when it saw Him coming; it immediately stopped!

I recall a situation where another pastor and I went to talk to a famous Gospel artist about a music project. He was a very feminine, metro sexual individual, but when we started talking with him, his whole disposition changed to that of a masculine man. He began to speak and act like a man for the entire time we conversed with him, but as soon as we finished he went back to his feminine ways.

I believe that we can have such an anointing on us that when drama sees us, it will want nothing to do with us because of the anointing. Our anointing identifies us to others, but how do we identify ourselves the drama in ourselves?

When we see drama in ourselves, what do we see? More importantly, what do we do about what we see?

Romans 7:21 (KJV) 21I find then a law, that, when I would do good, evil is present with me.

Psalm 51:5 (KJV) 5Behold, I was shapen in iniquity; and in sin did my mother conceive me.

Romans 7:24 (KJV) 24O wretched man that I am! who shall deliver me from the body of this death?

These passages point out the struggle that we all face with the drama that is within us; the struggle to do good when evil is always present. We don't want the drama, but yet here it is! It is either who we are by nature (how we were born) or who we are by nurture (how we were formed); more than likely a combination of the both.

Romans 7:25 (KJV) 25 I thank God through Jesus Christ our Lord. So then with the mind I myself serve the law of God; but with the flesh the law of sin.

Paul reveals here that we have an answer; and it is in the power of God. When we meditate on the Word of God, and walk in the Spirit of God; we develop an anointing to defeat the drama in us. We are able to tell ourselves, "don't even try it! I've been fasting too much, prayed too much, studied the word too much, praised God too much, and gained too much faith to let you stop me!"

The Identity of Knowledge

Some people fail to develop immunity to drama because they don't know the drama that they are dealing with; they simply lack the knowledge. They know that it is drama they know it's causing them hell, they know that it keeps them frustrated, aggravated, and discombobulated; but they just can't seem to get a handle on it, so that they can find relief.

They try to be nice, but nothing changes; they try counseling, but nothing changes; they try doing good, but always end up with the same old drama. They go to church, pray, and praise God; but still drama!

In Luke 8:30, Jesus asked the man that was possessed with demons (drama), "What is thy name?" In other words, "What am I dealing with?"

Am I dealing with territorial drama from principalities, personal or individual drama from powers, worldly drama of temptations from the rulers of darkness, or religious or church drama from spiritual wickedness in high places?

People die all the time because of misdiagnoses; and the main reason for misdiagnoses is when they treat the symptoms rather than the causes. Most people treat stomach pain with Pepto-Bismol, Maalox, or Pepcid Complete. What if the pain is not coming from an upset stomach, but a stomach ulcer? They may get temporarily relief from the pain (symptom), but nothing is done for the ulcer (cause). When the cause goes untreated, it develops into cancer.

The enemy will have us treating symptoms for temporary relief, but our cause is going untreated and getting even worse.

A territorial principality attacks us so we leave for temporary relief, but we haven't treated the cause or defeated the drama. So it gets worse!

An individual power attacks our relationship so we fight back, but we haven't treated the cause or defeated the drama. So it gets worse!

Spiritual wickedness creates church hurt, so we stop going to church, but we haven't treated the cause or defeated the drama. So it gets worse!

If the drama is coming from powers, then the answer is not to fight back, but to stop taking it personally because it is not about us. If the drama is coming from principalities, then the answer is to stop running and wait for your blessing. If the drama is coming from worldly temptations, then the answer is to mortify or deny your flesh by walking and growing in the Spirit of God. If the drama is coming from spiritual wickedness, then the answer is developing more patience until these spiritual forces are defeated.

The Bible teaches us that we are destroyed for a lack of knowledge. If we have the knowledge, then we can't be destroyed for a lack of it!

The Identity Of Power

Luke 8:28 (KJV) ^{28}*When he saw Jesus, he cried out, and fell down before him, and with a loud voice said, What have I to do with thee, Jesus, thou Son of God most high? I beseech thee, torment me not.*

When this man saw Jesus, he didn't just see a man in the natural; he saw the power of God in the spiritual. Every born again believer must understand the power of God in them, and then allow it to grow in them so that drama will see and recognize your power before it sees and recognizes you.

Luke 10:19 (KJV) ^{19}*Behold, I give unto you power to tread on serpents and scorpions, and over all the power of the enemy: and nothing shall by any means hurt you.*

Although drama may have a legion of spirits behind it, we have an anointing behind us that's even greater. The spirit that is in us is greater than the forces that are in the world. This is why Paul told Timothy to stir up the gift of God which is in him because God has not given us the spirit of fear, but of power, love, and a sound mind (2 Timothy 1:6-7).

If you really want to know just how powerful your anointing is, just look at the amount of drama coming your way!

1 Corinthians 10:13 (KJV) 13There hath no temptation taken you but such as is common to man: but God is faithful, who will not suffer you to be tempted above that ye are able; but will with the temptation also make a way to escape, that ye may be able to bear it.

Simply put, if it's coming your way, you already have an anointing for it! You have an anointing for every lie, an anointing for every betrayal, an anointing for every time they talk about you, an anointing for everyone that walked out on you, an anointing for every church hurt, an anointing for every time they passed you over, and an anointing for every time they said no!

As long as we have the power of God we have the promises of God; and no matter what drama comes our way, we can stand on His promises.

2 Corinthians 1:20 (KJV) [20]For all the promises of God in him are yea, and in him Amen, unto the glory of God by us.

Immunity From The Insanity Of Drama

Insanity or madness is the behavior whereby a person flouts (disobeys or ignores) societal norms and becomes a danger to themselves and others. A Latin phrase for insanity is "non compos mentis": a mind that is not composed. Drama, if not handled properly, has the capacity to literally drive us insane; "non compos mentis", a mind that is no longer composed; a mind that has been driven out of sanity.

Earlier when we studied the story of the man who called himself "Legion" (Mark 5:1-5); we found a man who had no discipline or self control. He was naked, living in a graveyard without any concern for himself or others around him. He was cutting himself; a form of self mutilation which is a psychological act of releasing pain. Just as depression can be described as anguish, suffering, torment turned inward, self-mutilation (cutting) can be described as psychological pain turned inward in the most physical way.

All of this physical and psychological behavior demonstrates a man that is struggling with his sanity; literally going insane as a result of depression, oppression, and possession of unclean spirits.

Another definition of insanity is doing the same thing over and over and expecting different results.

This is also a possible explanation for the condition of this man. Let's look again at the 12th chapter of Matthew.

Matthew 12:43-45 (KJV) *43When the unclean spirit is gone out of a man, he walketh through dry places, seeking rest, and findeth none. 44Then he saith, I will return into my house from whence I came out; and when he is come, he findeth it empty, swept, and garnished. 45Then goeth he, and taketh with himself seven other spirits more wicked than himself, and they enter in and dwell there: and the last state of that man is worse than the first. Even so shall it be also unto this wicked generation.*

Going through the same thing, doing the same thing, struggling with the same thing can literally drive us crazy. It will take the power of God to keep us sane in the midst of the insanity of the drama all around us.

Temporary Insanity (Explosive Drama)

The notion of temporary insanity argues that an otherwise sane individual can be driven to a state of insanity temporarily. Meaning although someone commits an egregious act, they cannot be held responsible because the insanity was temporary. This was first used as a legal defense by U.S. Congressman Daniel Sickles of New York in 1859 after he had killed his wife's lover.

The reality of life is that most of us are vulnerable to temporary insanity. It happens as a result of things just building and building, creating more and more pressure, until we just explode. It's like boiling food on a stove with a lid on the top of it. Everything starts out in a stable cool state. When you add heat to it the heat changes the state of both the food and the water. But because of the lid, pressure builds up and without relief, it explodes. Our response is to immediately remove the pot from the stove and remove it from the heat that caused the explosion, but since the food has not finished cooking, we still need the heat.

Here's where the insanity comes in: because the food is not done, we put it back on the same stove, the same heat, and it explodes again. However, this time it explodes even quicker because the food is still hot from the last time it was on the stove. Removing the pot from the heat simply treated the symptom, but did not fix the problem; and things simply get worse and worse.

One solution is to remove the lid to keep it from exploding, but then you will get a mess on the stove as everything is just constantly boiling over. So we have a conundrum or dilemma; if we remove the food from the heat, it won't finish cooking; if we keep it on the stove with a lid, the pressure will buildup and cause an explosion; and if we remove the lid, we will have a mess as the food spills over on the stove.

To further complicate matters, we actually need the two things that are causing us the problems; the heat from the stove and the pressure from the lid. The heat transforms or changes the state of things. It transforms cold water to boiling water and undesirable hard food that is useless, to desirable soft food that is useful. The lid not only keeps the food from boiling over creating a mess, it causes a buildup of pressure which actually causes the cooking process to happen even faster.

Biblically, we need heat to transform us as Christians, and pressure to speed up the process.

Romans 12:1-2 (KJV) 1I beseech you therefore, brethren, by the mercies of God, that ye present your bodies a living sacrifice, holy, acceptable unto God, which is your reasonable service. 2And be not conformed to this world: but be ye transformed by the renewing of your mind, that ye may prove what is that good, and acceptable, and perfect, will of God.

1 Corinthians 3:1-2 (KJV) 1And I, brethren, could not speak unto you as unto spiritual, but as unto carnal, even as unto babes in Christ. 2I have fed you with milk, and not with meat: for hitherto ye were not able to bear it, neither yet now are ye able.

How do we resolve our dilemma of heat and pressure? We need the heat to transform us, but it's causing us to boil over and create a mess. We need the pressure to quickly mature us, but it's causing us to explode. The answer is a pressure cooker. A pressure cooker will lock the mess in, but has a valve to release the pressure just before it explodes.

1 Peter 1:7 (KJV) ⁷That the trial of your faith, being much more precious than of gold that perisheth, though it be tried with fire, might be found unto praise and honor and glory at the appearing of Jesus Christ:

1 Corinthians 10:13 (KJV) 13There hath no temptation taken you but such as is common to man: but God is faithful, who will not suffer you to be tempted above that ye are able; but will with the temptation also make a way to escape, that ye may be able to bear it.

Matthew 11:28 (KJV) 28Come unto me, all ye that labor and are heavy laden, and I will give you rest.

Our relationship with God puts us in a spiritual pressure cooker. The heat of relationships with people transforms us, while the faithfulness of God protects us. It protects us by making sure that the enemy can't put more pressure on us than what we can handle. God does this by giving us a spiritual release valve of rest. Every time we get to the point where we feel like we just can't take it anymore, God gives us rest and the pressure is released. Regardless of what the enemy tells us, we can handle the heat, and we can handle the pressure; we are immune from the temporary insanity of relationships.

Environmental Insanity (Nurtured Drama)

Environment insanity is when environmental issues cause stress disorders. There are two forms of environmental insanity and they are commonly known as Battle Fatigue (Shellshock) and Post Traumatic Stress Disorder.

Battle Fatigue (Shellshock) is a military term used to categorize a range of behaviors resulting from the stress of battle which decreases the combatant's fighting efficiency. The most common symptoms are fatigue, slower reaction times, indecision, disconnection from one's surroundings, and inability to prioritize.

Daniel 7:25 (KJV) 25And he shall speak great words against the most High, and shall wear out the saints of the most High, and think to change times and laws: and they shall be given into his hand until a time and times and the dividing of time.

Mark 4:19 (KJV) 19And the cares of this world, and the deceitfulness of riches, and the lusts of other things entering in, choke the word, and it becometh unfruitful.

The interesting thing about battle fatigue is the greater the intensity of the fighting, the greater the ratio of battle fatigue casualties. However, the very nature of battle fatigue gives us the solution to it. Its nature is that it is transitory (not persistent, passes away). The answer to anything that is transitory, is patience or longsuffering.

Galatians 5:22 (KJV) 22But the fruit of the Spirit is love, joy, peace, longsuffering, ...

James 1:2-3 (KJV) 2My brethren, count it all joy when ye fall into divers temptations; 3Knowing this, that the trying of your faith worketh patience.

Isaiah 40:31 (KJV) 31But they that wait upon the LORD shall renew their strength; they shall mount up with wings as eagles; they shall run, and not be weary; and they shall walk, and not faint.

Post Traumatic Stress Disorder (PTSD) is an anxiety disorder that can develop after exposure to terrifying events that threatened or caused grave harm. Unlike battle fatigue, it is not transitory, but a severe and ongoing emotional reaction to extreme trauma; a constant threat to physical or psychological integrity, overwhelming the psychological defenses.

Some people have been through so much hell for so long that they just can't seem to break free of it. Years later they are still struggling with PTSD.

Psalm 51: 5Behold, I was shapen in iniquity; and in sin did my mother conceive me.

There are some things you can't counsel your way out of, you can't wait your way out of, you can't hope, wish, love, or buy your way out of. The answer to PTSD is to PRAY!

Matthew 17:21 (KJV) 21Howbeit this kind goeth not out but by prayer and fasting.

Luke 18:1 (KJV) 1... men ought always to pray, and not to faint;

James 5:16 (KJV) 16... The effectual fervent prayer of a righteous man availeth much.

Psalm 51:10-12 (KJV) 10Create in me a clean heart, O God; and renew a right spirit within me. 11Cast me not away from thy presence; and take not thy holy spirit from me. 12Restore unto me the joy of thy salvation; and uphold me with thy free spirit.

Regardless of our environment, how we were born and how we were formed, we are immune from environmental insanity because we have "patience" and we have "prayer". When we combine "patience" and "prayer" in our relationships, we become "Pushers". PUSH is an acronym for "pray until something happens"; so when the enemy attacks us with the environmental insanity of PTSD, we PUSH!

Immunity From Generational Insanity

What do we do about generational curses, insanity, and drama that are internal or hereditary? It is not temporary, transitory, environmental, or external; it's a part of us. How do you deal with something that is part of you?

Romans 7:18-21 (KJV) [18]*For I know that in me (that is, in my flesh,) dwelleth no good thing: for to will is present with me; but how to perform that which is good I find not.* [19]*For the good that I would I do not: but the evil which I would not, that I do.* [20]*Now if I do that I would not, it is no more I that do it, but sin that dwelleth in me.* [21]*I find then a law, that, when I would do good, evil is present with me.*

Generational drama is the struggle that we have with sins of compulsive behavior. People who struggle with conditions like kleptomania (the impulse to steal), obsessive compulsive behaviors, and even certain preferences many times have them at birth. Even some addictive behaviors and sexual tendencies towards homosexuality and effeminacy in men can be traced back well before the age of consent or accountability.

Some people believe God is perfect and therefore can't create anything this is not perfect. He did not create anything that was not perfect, He will take that which is imperfect and corrupt so that it becomes perfect.

John 9:1-5 (KJV) ¹And as Jesus passed by, he saw a man which was blind from his birth. ²And his disciples asked him, saying, Master, who did sin, this man, or his parents, that he was born blind? ³Jesus answered, Neither hath this man sinned, nor his parents: but that the works of God should be made manifest in him. ⁴I must work the works of him that sent me, while it is day: the night cometh, when no man can work. ⁵As long as I am in the world, I am the light of the world.

If people can be born blind or deaf, then they can be born with any generational condition that is not perfect. This is what is known a generational curses, insanity, or drama. The solution is not to accept the condition we find ourselves in but to use the power of God to change it!

Born This Way, Reborn God's Way

Some people say I'm like this because of my heritage. I was born this way; I inherited it from my family. Many of us know some families where it appears that just about everybody in the family suffers from the same thing. A family where everybody is hot tempered, everybody flies off the handle, or everybody is depressed; a family where it seems that every marriage ends in divorce, abuse, and hurt. It appears that everyone has the same curses, same insanity, and same drama.

Exodus 20:5 (KJV) ⁵Thou shalt not bow down thyself to them, nor serve them: for I the LORD thy God am a jealous God, visiting the iniquity of the fathers upon the children unto the third and fourth generation of them that hate me;

One of the main problems we run into when it comes to generational drama is denial. We deny that we even have a problem. In the 51ˢᵗ Psalm, David acknowledges that he was born and shaped with problems.

Psalm 51:5 (KJV) ⁵Behold, I was shapen in iniquity; and in sin did my mother conceive me.

Then there is the denial of how we got the problem. This is the argument of whether a person was born with a certain condition or chose it. However, this is a useless argument. If you are in a sewer filled with waste, how you got in it is irrelevant to how you get out of it. You could have jumped in by choice, been tricked to get in, pushed in through deception, or you could have been born in it through no effort of your own. It does not matter. The only thing that matters is how to get out!

The enemy will use denial to get us to accept our problems. He convinces us that it's not a problem, it's not our fault; we were born this way and we can't help it. The enemy has us ask ourselves, if we were born this way, how can it be wrong? It is wrong and it is wrong because of our flesh and the lust of the flesh that cause us to fail.

James 1:13-17 (KJV) [13]*Let no man say when he is tempted, I am tempted of God: for God cannot be tempted with evil, neither tempteth he any man:* [14]*But every man is tempted, when he is drawn away of his own lust, and enticed.* [15]*Then when lust hath conceived, it bringeth forth sin: and sin, when it is finished, bringeth forth death.* [16]*Do not err, my beloved brethren.* [17]*Every good gift and every perfect gift is from above, and cometh down from the Father of lights, with whom is no variableness, neither shadow of turning.*

We must deny ourselves and our flesh or we will lose our soul.

Matthew 16:23-26 (KJV) [23]*But he turned, and said unto Peter, Get thee behind me, Satan: thou art an offence unto me: for thou savourest not the things that be of God, but those that be of men.* [24]*Then said Jesus unto his disciples, If any man will come after me, let him deny himself, and take up his cross, and follow me.* [25]*For whosoever will save his life shall lose it: and whosoever will lose his life for my sake shall find it.* [26]*For what is a man profited, if he shall gain the whole world, and lose his own soul? or what shall a man give in exchange for his soul?*

Once we deny ourselves, we then ask God to purge or wash us out, then create a completely new heart.

Psalm 51:5-10 (KJV) [5]Behold, I was shapen in iniquity; and in sin did my mother conceive me. [6]Behold, thou desirest truth in the inward parts: and in the hidden part thou shalt make me to know wisdom. [7]Purge me with hyssop, and I shall be clean: wash me, and I shall be whiter than snow. [8]Make me to hear joy and gladness; that the bones which thou hast broken may rejoice. [9]Hide thy face from my sins, and blot out all mine iniquities. [10]Create in me a clean heart, O God; and renew a right spirit within me.

John 3:1-8 (KJV) [1]There was a man of the Pharisees, named Nicodemus, a ruler of the Jews: [2]The same came to Jesus by night, and said unto him, Rabbi, we know that thou art a teacher come from God: for no man can do these miracles that thou doest, except God be with him. [3]Jesus answered and said unto him, Verily, verily, I say unto thee, Except a man be born again, he cannot see the kingdom of God. [4]Nicodemus saith unto him, How can a man be born when he is old? can he enter the second time into his mother's womb, and be born? [5]Jesus answered, Verily, verily, I say unto thee, Except a man be born of water and of the Spirit, he cannot enter into the kingdom of God. ⁶That which is born of the flesh is flesh; and that which is born of the Spirit is spirit. ⁷Marvel not that I said unto thee, Ye must be born again. ⁸The wind bloweth where it listeth, and thou hearest the sound thereof, but canst not tell whence it cometh, and whither it goeth: so is every one that is born of the Spirit.

Breaking The Generational Cycle

One of the things we must understand about generational curses, insanity, and drama is that every generation gets worse and worse. We learn about the generational progression of wickedness in the 12ᵗʰ chapter of Matthew.

Matthew 12:43-45 (KJV) ⁴³When the unclean spirit is gone out of a man, he walketh through dry places, seeking rest, and findeth none. ⁴⁴Then he saith, I will return into my house from whence I came out; and when he is come, he findeth it empty, swept, and garnished. ⁴⁵Then goeth he, and taketh with himself seven other spirits more wicked than himself, and they enter in and dwell there: and the last state of that man is worse than the first. Even so shall it be also unto this wicked generation.

As Christians we have the capacity to break the cycle of generational curses. We can break the cycle of hate, depression, curses, poverty, and drama by becoming a new creature.

2 Corinthians 5:17 (KJV) 17Therefore if any man be in Christ, he is a new creature: old things are passed away; behold, all things are become new.

We can break the cycle by becoming a child of God:

1 John 3:2 (KJV) 2Beloved, now are we the sons of God, and it doth not yet appear what we shall be: but we know that, when he shall appear, we shall be like him; for we shall see him as he is.

We can break the cycle by becoming a joint-heir with Christ:

Romans 8:14-18 (KJV) 14For as many as are led by the Spirit of God, they are the sons of God. 15For ye have not received the spirit of bondage again to fear; but ye have received the Spirit of adoption, whereby we cry, Abba, Father. 16The Spirit itself beareth witness with our spirit, that we are the children of God: 17And if children, then heirs; heirs of God, and joint-heirs with Christ; if so be that we suffer with him, that we may be also glorified together. 18For I reckon that the sufferings of this present time are not worthy to be compared with the glory which shall be revealed in us.

The Resilience to Bounce Back

The man who called himself Legion should have never survived his experience with the legion of demons that possessed him. Their ultimate goal was to destroy him.

Mark 5:9-15 (KJV) ⁹And he asked him, What is thy name? And he answered, saying, My name is Legion: for we are many. ¹⁰And he besought him much that he would not send them away out of the country. ¹¹Now there was there nigh unto the mountains a great herd of swine feeding. ¹²And all the devils besought him, saying, Send us into the swine, that we may enter into them. ¹³And forthwith Jesus gave them leave. And the unclean spirits went out, and entered into the swine: and the herd ran violently down a steep place into the sea, (they were about two thousand;) and were choked in the sea. ¹⁴And they that fed the swine fled, and told it in the city, and in the country. And they went out to see what it was that was done. ¹⁵And they come to Jesus, and see him that was possessed with the devil, and had the legion, sitting, and clothed, and in his right mind: and they were afraid.

By all accounts, this man should have been physically, emotionally, & spiritually dead. Physically he was bound with chains and shackles, but would constantly break out of them; unable to be tamed, and constantly in physical pain. Emotionally he was on the edge of insanity disobeying and ignoring societal norms, becoming a danger to himself and others; always crying and cutting himself. Based on what the legion of unclean spirits did to the herd of swine after they left the man, it is clear that their intent was to kill him.

Now imagine these two contrasting images: A man swaying from depression to insanity, out of his mind, a danger to himself and other, crazy, naked, living in a grave yard and on the other hand, a man sitting, clothed, and in his right mind. What is it that caused this man to rebound from insanity to a sound mind; from near death to life? Resilience!

Resilience is the capability or capacity to withstand shock without being permanently deformed or ruptured. It is the ability to recover from or adjust easily to misfortune or change. Resilience is also the capability of a strained body to recover its size and shape after deformation caused especially by compressive stress.

Perhaps you are familiar with the plane crash of US Airways Flight 1549 in New York; often referred to as the Miracle on the Hudson. After being struck by a flock of birds, the pilot with both engines out, maneuvered the plane through the city and ditched the plane in the Hudson River, saving all 155 people on board.

How does a pilot maneuver an 80 ton metal bus that loses both engines at 3000 feet, flying over the most populated city in the world, land in a narrow river, and not one of the 155 passengers die? It was a miracle, but the miracle happened before the accident happened.

The flight was piloted by Captain Sullenberger, the most uniquely qualified pilot; who specialized and taught other captains about safety. Captain Sullenberger also happened to be a glider pilot who knew how to fly a plane without power. Since the incident happened at 3000 feet, it gave him enough time to land in the Hudson River. If it happened at a higher elevation, the plane would have been over the Atlantic Ocean. If it happened at a lower elevation, they would have crashed into a building. There were ferries, tug boats, and emergency personnel who responded within minutes.

The miracle was the resilience God put in place before the drama ever happened. The pilot, the plane, the training, and the first responders all contributed to what we saw take place on that day. It was the resilience to respond and bounce back that made the difference!

We are all walking miracles because God has put resilience in us. He has already prepared us to jump back; recoil to get back up again, and bounce back from everything the enemy throws our way.

Bend But Don't Break

Resilience is flexibility, the ability to bend, but don't break. The reason why things break is because they are inflexible; they represent the antonym or opposite of resilience which is rigidity.

Rigidity means to be devoid of flexibility, inflexible, a rigid bar of metal, stiff and unyielding. Spiritual rigidity represents religious folks who are so spiritually rigid or deep, that they are no earthly good.

2 Timothy 3:5 (KJV) 5Having a form of godliness, but denying the power thereof: from such turn away.

What makes them spiritually rigid is because they break instead of bend when pressure is applied or drama shows up. In order to bend and not break, one must transform from rigidity to flexibility. This transformation occurs under heat.

1 Peter 1:7 (KJV) 7That the trial of your faith, being much more precious than of gold that perisheth, though it be tried with fire, might be found unto praise and honour and glory at the appearing of Jesus Christ:

The heat of drama transforms us so that we become flexible. This happens because heat activates the Holy Spirit in us to produce fruit.

Galatians 5:22-23 (KJV) 22But the fruit of the Spirit is love, joy, peace, longsuffering, gentleness, goodness, faith, 23Meekness, temperance: against such there is no law.

The heat of hatred produces love, the heat of disappointment produces joy, the heat of confusion produces peace, and the heat of not getting what we want produces longsuffering. So when the pressure is applied, we bend but don't break.

Drama may bend us out of shape, but we bend and don't break because we have the resilience to bounce back!

Sink But Don't Drown

Resilience is also buoyancy, the ability to sink but not drown. The reason why things sink is because they have no capacity to float; they are characterized by spiritual submergence.

Submergence means to sink, to go to the bottom, to become buried; to fall or drop to a lower place or level, to disappear from view. Spiritual submergence is characterized by being in the flesh.

1 Corinthians 3:1-3 (KJV) 1And I, brethren, could not speak unto you as unto spiritual, but as unto carnal, even as unto babes in Christ. 2I have fed you with milk, and not with meat: for hitherto ye were not able to bear it, neither yet now are ye able. 3For ye are yet carnal: for whereas there is among you envying, and strife, and divisions, are ye not carnal, and walk as men?

Hebrews 12:1-3 (KJV) 1Wherefore seeing we also are compassed about with so great a cloud of witnesses, let us lay aside every weight, and the sin which doth so easily beset us, and let us run with patience the race that is set before us, 2Looking unto Jesus the author and finisher of our faith; who for the joy that was set before him endured the cross, despising the shame, and is set down at the right hand of the throne of God. 3For consider him that endured such contradiction of sinners against himself, lest ye be wearied and faint in your minds.

Buoyancy is the tendency of a body to float or to rise when submerged in a fluid. The power of a fluid to exert an upward force on a body placed in it. The ability to recover quickly from depression or discouragement; to maintain at a high level!

Lose But Don't Lose It

Resilience is the ability to lose, but not "lose it'. The enemy uses the drama of loss to try to get us to lose it. He'll use disappointment to get us to lose our hope, but we have resilience in our faith which is the substance of things hoped for. Drama can bring us frustration and depression to make us sad, but we know that the joy of the Lord is our strength. People will betray us to get us to lose our trust, but resilience is knowing that our trust is to be in the Lord who directs our path. The enemy will use hatred to get us to lose our love, but in God we know that love conquerors a multitude of evil.

Spiritual resilience is the ability to suffer loss, but not lose it. Everything that we lose is connected to the flesh, but since we are spiritual, we bounce back!

Luke 9:23-24 (KJV) 23And he said to them all, If any man will come after me, let him deny himself, and take up his cross daily, and follow me. 24For whosoever will save his life shall lose it: but whosoever will lose his life for my sake, the same shall save it.

John 4:23-24 (KJV) 23But the hour cometh, and now is, when the true worshippers shall worship the Father in spirit and in truth: for the Father seeketh such to worship him. 24God is a Spirit: and they that worship him must worship him in spirit and in truth.

1 John 4:4 (KJV) 4Ye are of God, little children, and have overcome them: because greater is he that is in you, than he that is in the world.

Because of the God in us we bounce back from ridicule, from betrayal, lies, hatred, and anything the enemy throws at us.

The Resilience to Bounce Back From The World

How much hell must have this man Legion been through from the world? How many bad relationships? How many personal and emotional struggles? How much drama from the cares of this world?

Mark 4:19 (KJV) ¹⁹And the cares of this world, and the deceitfulness of riches, and the lusts of other things entering in, choke the word, and it becometh unfruitful.

If we are not careful, the world will get us in trouble. Doing everything to keep up with what the world defines as success. They tell us what we have to drive, what kind of house to live in, what to look like. We kill ourselves trying to keep up by spending money we don't have, to by things we don't need, to impress people we don't even like. Often we feel depressed because of a job, the lack of money, because we are not in a particular group or clique; doing everything we can to become accepted by others.

When Bernard L. Madoff "made off" with over 50 billion dollars in a ponzi scheme; one of his victims killed himself. He allowed what he had to become who he was; so that when he lost what he had, he lost himself. We must never allow what we do, what we have, or who we are with to become who we are. We can always get another job, get more stuff, or even get more friends, but we can never get another soul.

1 John 2:15-16 (KJV) [15]Love not the world, neither the things that are in the world. If any man love the world, the love of the Father is not in him. [16]For all that is in the world, the lust of the flesh, and the lust of the eyes, and the pride of life, is not of the Father, but is of the world.

This passage of scripture explains a fundamental difference between true saints and the world; and that is how we perceive life. The world perceives life through their eyes and is controlled by their emotions. The eyes are the window to the soul (mind, will, emotions); what a person thinks, how they feel, and what they do. The eyes see and translate to thoughts; thoughts become emotions; and emotions become actions. So when a person mistreats you and says, "I don't know why I did that"; the reason is because they were thinking it; then they felt it; lastly something triggered the opportunity for them to do it!

This also explains why people hate and/or mistreat you when then don't even know you. It's not you it's what they see in you.

1 Samuel 8:7 (KJV) [7]And the LORD said unto Samuel, Hearken unto the voice of the people in all that they say unto thee: for they have not rejected thee, but they have rejected me, that I should not reign over them.

John 15:18-19 (KJV) ¹⁸*If the world hate you, ye know that it hated me before it hated you.* ¹⁹*If ye were of the world, the world would love his own: but because ye are not of the world, but I have chosen you out of the world, therefore the world hateth you.*

John 15:25 (KJV) ²⁵*But this cometh to pass, that the word might be fulfilled that is written in their law, They hated me without a cause.*

They see and hate the God in you. When they see you, they see your anointing, they see your favor!

Genesis 37:3-4 (KJV) ³*Now Israel loved Joseph more than all his children, because he was the son of his old age: and he made him a coat of many colours.* ⁴*And when his brethren saw that their father loved him more than all his brethren, they hated him, and could not speak peaceably unto him.*

The world perceives through their eyes and are controlled by their emotions, but we perceive through the Spirit and are controlled by our Faith!

2 Corinthians 5:7 (KJV) ⁷*(For we walk by faith, not by sight:)*

The world walks by what they see, we walk by what we believe! They use their eyes, we use our ears. They see what Satan is showing them, but we hear what God is revealing to us!

Romans 10:17 (KJV) [17]*So then faith cometh by hearing, and hearing by the word of God.*

This is why the world can't figure us out. They can't see it, but we can hear it! It is about something we heard in the Word; something we heard from the Pastor.

We bounce back from the world by hearing and believing the Word of God.

The Resilience to Bounce Back From Self

The reality of our existence: dealing with relationships, family, church, and even our calling is that many times we can be our own worst enemies. If we would be honest with ourselves, we have gotten ourselves in more trouble than anybody else. Why? We have been with ourselves longer than anyone else has been.

How much hell did "Legion" put himself through? The Bible clearly indicates that we can be our own worst enemy.

Romans 7:18-21 (KJV) [18]For I know that in me (that is, in my flesh,) dwelleth no good thing: for to will is present with me; but how to perform that which is good I find not. [19]For the good that I would I do not: but the evil which I would not, that I do. [20]Now if I do that I would not, it is no more I that do it, but sin that dwelleth in me. [21]I find then a law, that, when I would do good, evil is present with me.

Jeremiah 17:9 (KJV) [9]The heart is deceitful above all things, and desperately wicked: who can know it?

How do we get to the point where we give ourselves so much drama? Is it nature or nurture?

Some people believe that it is nature; generational, in our DNA.

Exodus 20:5 (KJV) ⁵Thou shalt not bow down thyself to them, nor serve them: for I the LORD thy God am a jealous God, visiting the iniquity of the fathers upon the children unto the third and fourth generation of them that hate me;

Others believe that we are in this condition because of nurture; how the environment shaped us. This would explain why hurt people hurt and abused people abuse. The 51ˢᵗ Psalm lead us to conclude that it is a little of both!

Psalm 51:5 (KJV) ⁵Behold, I was shapen in iniquity; and in sin did my mother conceive me.

To argue Nature or Nurture to me is a "Red Herring"; in other words, a useless argument that misses the point. If you are in a mess, your goal is not to argue how I got in it, but how to get out of it. Whether you accidentally fell in, were intentionally pushed in, or were in it from birth because that's where your mother was; has nothing to do with how you get out of it. Our goal should always be how to get out of the condition we find ourselves in. And the bible gives us the answer.

2 Corinthians 5:17 (KJV) *17Therefore if any man be in Christ, he is a new creature: old things are passed away; behold, all things are become new.*

It does not matter how you were born, you must be born again. The key to having the resilience to bounce back from self is in learning how to denying self.

Luke 9:23-24 (KJV) *23And he said to them all, If any man will come after me, let him deny himself, and take up his cross daily, and follow me. 24For whosoever will save his life shall lose it: but whosoever will lose his life for my sake, the same shall save it.*

Everyone must understand that within every creature is the innate desire for self-preservation; but not just the desire to preserve one's physical life, but to also preserve their feelings, dignity, and emotions. They fight back when they are threatened; push back when pushed; hate back when hated. If they are not treating us right, we leave; leaving our jobs with no job; leaving marriages with no counseling; leaving churches without talking to the pastor.

God wants us to deny ourselves so that we can strengthen ourselves.

2 Corinthians 12:8-10 (KJV) *8For this thing I besought the Lord thrice, that it might depart from me.*

⁹And he said unto me, My grace is sufficient for thee: for my strength is made perfect in weakness. Most gladly therefore will I rather glory in my infirmities, that the power of Christ may rest upon me. ¹⁰Therefore I take pleasure in infirmities, in reproaches, in necessities, in persecutions, in distresses for Christ's sake: for when I am weak, then am I strong.

Galatians 5:22-23 (KJV) ²²But the fruit of the Spirit is love, joy, peace, longsuffering, gentleness, goodness, faith, ²³Meekness, temperance: against such there is no law.

The resilience to bounce back from self is to trust God, deny ourselves, and allow Him to build our spirit. If we pray for God to remove something and He doesn't, then He is using that thing to build us up. When we deny ourselves, it weakens our flesh so that God can strengthen our spirit. To give us more love, God sends someone to hate us. To give us more joy, God sends something to make us depressed. To give us more peace, God will allow everything to go crazy. The bottom line is God wants to strengthen us, renew us, build us to the point that we can bounce back from anything.

Psalm 51:10-12 (KJV) ¹⁰Create in me a clean heart, O God; and renew a right spirit within me. ¹¹Cast me not away from thy presence; and take not thy holy spirit from me. ¹²Restore unto me the joy of thy salvation; and uphold me with thy free spirit.

Psalm 51:10-12 (KJV) 10 Create in me a clean heart, O God; and renew a right spirit within me. 11Cast me not away from thy presence; and take not thy holy spirit from me. 12Restore unto me the joy of thy salvation; and uphold me with thy free spirit.

Now we have the power to look at ourselves and tell ourselves to get behind us. We bounce back from ourselves by denying ourselves.

PART 3: Solutions For Difficult and Challenging Relationships By Dr. Grace Nichols

Solutions For Relationships

Do you have challenges in your relationships? Are your relationships working for you? Well relationships are a part of God's design for our lives. No matter how successful we are in life, family or business, we will virtually be incomplete without healthy relationships.

During my Masters Degree coursework I had the opportunity to take a class on relationships. This class literally changed my life and the way I looked at relationships. It gave me an opportunity to view various studies and their outcomes. It gave me an opportunity to take a closer look at what various relationship experts thought on this subject. This has helped me tremendously in my pursuit of lifelong relationships.

Growing up I've always prayed that God would send someone in my life who would first be my best friend. That was important to me because I knew that was the foundation I needed to then build a marriage. Developing a relationship built on friendship was very important for me in my marriage relationship because no matter what challenges my husband and I faced, we would look at the covenant we made each other and not our problems. I would ask myself the question; was this misunderstanding so important that I would allow it to tear our relationship apart? The answer every time would be no. My relationship was built on a more firm foundation. When our friendship grew into a relationship, my best friend Wil gave me a friendship ring with my ruby birthstone for my pinky finger. This was not an engagement ring. It simply said I am serious about you. The next ring I received was an engagement ring, which meant you are the person I want to spend the rest of my life with. My husband Wil proposed to me after receiving the blessings of my Father, Mother and Pastor, my spiritual dad. This was the beginning of a lifelong relationship with the best friend I prayed to God for at an early age. My relationship with my husband means the world to me so I can't afford to let anything separate us. We have two beautiful kids that God has blessed us with, Anthony our oldest and Crystal our baby girl. They have both grown up and over the years my husband and I have developed a very close relationship with our son and daughter. There is a bond between us that runs deep. That bond keeps us accountable to God, because we made a covenant to train them up in the way they should go.

Researchers have conducted extensive studies on what makes people happy. The answer was not health, success, wealth, personal achievement or good looks but the clear winner was close relationships. We need love, affection, companionship, and a sense of belonging to thrive and survive. National surveys say: A quarter of all Americans have said they have felt lonely in the last month. Two-thirds of Americans say close relationships with other people are always on their minds.

Relationships have the capacity to take us on an emotional roller coaster ride. Why you might ask? Well, the people we love the most holds the greatest potential for causing us the most pain in our lives. Life matters and relationships matter. Pain has the propensity of strengthening our relationships and bringing us closer together. What we do today determine the relationships we have tomorrow. Everything we do in a relationship is an investment in the other person's life. We are in each other's life to make it better, not bitter. We must barrel through the hurt and the pain and do whatever we must to save our relationships. Relationships worth having are worth fighting for. The number-one reason college students seek counseling, in fact, is for their relationships.

God created both males and females for relationships. As we move through life and interact with others, we don't experience the same level of relationships with everyone we know. Sometimes, relationships just happen, such as being drawn to someone who enjoys the same lifestyle or hobby as you enjoy. Many factors determine the different levels of relationships we experience with the people in our lives. Most relationships take time to grow and develop. Some relationships develop a result of like interest, shared hurts, or shared joys. Relationships that last are built on emotional support for each other.

My marriage relationship with my husband would never grow deeper if we did not have an emotional bond. One that ties our soul, dreams hopes and aspirations together and placed us on the same path of this journey through life. Our marriage is fulfilled because we are emotionally connected. Our relationship took twenty years to get to the emotional level it is, so allow your relationship time to grow and develop. When you make a covenant make it for life and stay focused so that the storms of life won't discourage you. It is easy to get in and out of relationships but if you ever want to experience fulfillment in life it's the storms that make your relationship stronger not running away. I feel safe in my relationships when I can reveal what's inside of me, my thoughts and my feelings.

Relationships should be built with friends who can share your ideas, and philosophies, friends with whom you can grow intellectually. Friends should not only be able to stand by your side but also stand apart with an objective view. They should feel free to not side with you when you are in the wrong. A friend should take time to know you inside and out and appreciate your differences. A friend should be loyal and trustworthy. These are the qualities in which relationships should be built on. Loyalty requires that your friend sticks with you no matter what.

Proverbs 17:17 says "A friend loves at all time, and a brother is born for adversity".

The book of proverbs speaks on relationships and gives practical principles for everyday life. It addresses issues such as the fleeting nature of friendship built on the external values that we pursue today, such as power, wealth or position.

Proverbs 19:4-7 NASB, says, Wealth brings many friends, but a poor man's friend deserts him. A false witness will not go unpunished, and he who pours out lies will not go free. Many curry favor with a ruler, and everyone is the friend of a man who gives gifts. A poor man is shunned by all his relatives – how much more do his friends avoid him!

Take time to invest in others and watch your life become more enriched and fulfilled. What you do today will determine the quality of your relationships tomorrow. Live your life to the fullest and treasure your friendships.

Philippians 1:6 (KJV) says, ⁶Being confident of this very thing, that he which hath begun a good work in you will perform it until the day of Jesus Christ:

Relationships can be very rewarding. It can stimulate growth spiritually, emotionally and mentally. Friends challenge you to think and thus grow in so many areas of your life.

Proverbs 27:17, NASB says *"As iron sharpens irons, so one man sharpens another."*

Relationships can be expressed in two different ways, through our actions or through our words. I often say to my husband Wil, I am not in your life to tear you down but to build you up. We need to be a source of encouragement to our friends, because encouragement breeds confidence. We have to look at our relationship as having worth and dignity. We never get rid of things that we value dearly. Anything that we value defines us and brings a level of security, for example a nice home in a nice neighborhood or a beautiful car. As Christians we don't pick or choose who we encourage. Whoever we are in relationship with it is our duty to encourage them on a regular basis.

I Thessalonians 5:11 NASB Paul wrote, *"Therefore encourage one another and build each other up, just as in fact you are doing".*

"Encourage" is from a Greek work "Parakaleo" meaning, to come alongside and console, cheer up, comfort or help someone else. We are to build up others who don't have confidence in themselves. In Thessalonians 5:14 NASB Paul again tells us to encourage the timid – those who are discouraged and looks like they are ready to throw in the towel or give up on life. We must share our faith and our hope with those we are in relationship with. We must help those who can't help themselves that is our Christian duty.

That is the assignment we have and the covenant we make when we are in relationship with others. When we are going through our valley experiences, it is those times that we can appreciate the value of a true friend's helping hand to help keep us on the right track. When you have a Christian friend you have the extra benefit of being able to discuss spiritual issues, pray for one another and thereby grow spiritually. Spiritual growth is a deeper level of growth and more fulfilling, it is by far one of the greatest elements of a strong relationship you can ever experience in life.

Ecclesiates 4:10, KJV says "Woe to him who is alone when he falls and has not another to lift him up.

We were created by God for relationships. That is what makes our lives more fulfilling and more meaningful.

A survey was completed with the singles at our church (males and females) in North Carolina. One of their number one topics of interest was dealing with loneliness. One of the highlights of the session was exploring with our singles that you can be in a crowded room and still feel alone. Loneliness is a state of the mind. God did say in Genesis that "It was not good for man to be alone." That is why he was given a helpmate, a friend. Adam and Eve were not only in relationship and communion with God but with each other.

Many of us at some time in our lives have felt as though something is missing. All of us have struggled with loneliness. We all felt detached, unaccepted, separated from the group we'd like to be a part of. When we find ourselves in this empty space, we typically search outside ourselves, often compulsively for something or someone to fill it.

Some women when they become lonely they will find a mall or go shopping somewhere to fill that void, or eat chocolate, ice-cream or whatever they crave, or clean and/or reorganize the entire house. These are all distractions from the emptiness they feel on the inside or the rejection they receive from the outside.

In order to grow and develop in your relationships, you must establish a sense of confidence and completeness. You must establish respect for yourself, a healthy sense of self worth and a healthy sense of self-concept. You must know yourself and love yourself just as you are.

What Makes People Happy

In our church we have fellowship groups and the primary purpose is for the church body on a whole to be broken down into smaller more intimate special interest groups. We have discovered through our small groups more and more relationships are being developed because there is a connection with other like-minded people. It is only in the context of connection with others that our deepest needs can be met. That's what John Donne meant when he said "No man is an Island." We need love affection and camaraderie and a sense of belonging to survive.

We pull money from a machine and never interact with a human bank teller; we walk on a crowded sidewalk without connecting eyes with other pedestrians; we call telephone assistance only to get information from a computerized voice activated system.

A study showed World War II experiments of orphaned babies identified a fatal and mysterious disease called Marasmus. It was studied in a group of orphaned babies who were placed in a café facility with brightly colored toys, new furniture and good food. The pleasant accommodations, however, did not improve the lives of these children as their health rapidly deteriorated. They soon stopped playing with the new toys and gradually lost their appetites. Their tiny systems weakened, becoming lethargic and wearing down some children died.

After a short time of investigation, the doctors made a simple prescription, curing the problem within days. For ten minutes, each hour, all children were to be picked up by a nurse, hugged, kissed, played with, and talked to. With this simple prescription, the little ones brightened, their appetites returned, and they once again played with their toys. Their "marasmus" was cured.

Two independent studies were done at the University of California at Berkley and the University of Michigan. The results were that adults who do not cultivate nurture relationships have premature death rates twice as high as those who do.

The study indicates that social isolation is as significant to mortality as smoking is to high blood pressure, and high cholesterol is to obesity and lack of physical exercise.

Everyone in this life wants to be appreciated, admired, accepted, and loved. "Our need for relationship is all a part of God's design and master plan for humanity." We were created for relationships

Why Relationships Are So Complicated

Relationships become complicated because we can't understand the purpose behind the pain we feel stemming from the hurt caused by those who we hold dear. It is our dearest friend or loved one who holds the greatest potential for causing us the greatest pain. There is also the mystery of relating to the opposite sex. It is difficult for men to understand women and it is also difficult for women to understand men.

Folk wisdom raises more questions than give answers:
1. Do birds of a feather flock together, or do opposites attract
2. Does absence make the heart grow fonder, or is it out of sight, out of mind

It is true that opposites attract so it will require that both parties in the relationship work hard at developing open and honest communication. Communication or the lack thereof seems to be the fall of many potentially good relationships. That is the reason why there are so many workshops and seminars being offered on effective communication. Conflict arises when both parties in the relationship are not operating by the same rules and with the same understanding of each other's needs, wants and expectations.

Myths That Destroy Relationships

Attaching Ourselves To Others Will Fulfill Us

By attaching ourselves to someone, we assume will make us magically and spontaneously complete. We expect that all of our needs will be met. This is the wrong expectation to have because our fulfillment cannot be found in a man or in a woman. They are human and will fail us every time.

The Story of Angel and Tim: Angel in her mid twenties dated Tim a few times in college but nothing serious ever developed. Tim moved back to Washington DC because of a great job opportunity. Angel and Tim attended the same Family church and began to date. Angel thought that their relationship had grown to more than just friends. Tim was focused more on his career in Computer Engineering than his relationship with Angel. He was now considering a move to California to enroll in a training program that would make him more attractive to potential employers. That is what brought Angel to a Christian counselor.

Angel after six months of dating in Washington DC, she was considering moving to New York City to be with Tim. Her job was an entry level clerical position. Her aunt lived in California and had a guest room. Angel was going to move halfway across the country to be near a guy that made no commitment to their relationship. She thought: Maybe Tim and I are made for each other. If I am closer to him this will help me prove my love to him. We are meant for each other, he just doesn't know it yet. She thought something could really develop between them. The problem is, chasing after another person to have a relationship that makes you feel complete or better about your-self is a recipe for disaster.

Six months after her move, Angel showed up at the Christian Therapist's office. Things did not work out like she thought. Tim began dating another woman he met on the job. Angel was left with a terrible broken heart.

Too many people attach themselves to another person to obtain approval, affirmation, purpose, safety and identity. Self worth does not come from the existence or presence of someone in your life. Expecting another person, friend, partner, husband, or wife to provide you with completeness for your life is unrealistic and actually unfair. It isn't anyone else's job to give you an identity or makes you whole. People in your life should not have that much power over you. People in your life are meant to share it not be it.

Society and the use of technology have made it difficult for us to develop and maintain relationships especially in the service industry where tellers and retail personnel are being replaced by automated machines. We can now call 800 numbers or help desk for assistance with various products or for trouble shooting problems. This eliminates the personal contact needed to develop healthy relationships.

We learned the power of being touched, hugged, kissed, played with and talked to when doctors in World War II uncovered a fatal disease called marasmus. There is power in touching and being close to those who we have a permanent relationship with.

The bible gives us rules and instructions on relationships:

Colossians 3:18-25 (KJV) [18]*Wives, submit yourselves unto your own husbands, as it is fit in the Lord.* [19]*Husbands, love your wives, and be not bitter against them.* [20]*Children, obey your parents in all things: for this is well pleasing unto the Lord.* [21]*Fathers, provoke not your children to anger, lest they be discouraged.* [22]*Servants, obey in all things your masters according to the flesh; not with eyeservice, as menpleasers; but in singleness of heart, fearing God:* [23]*And whatsoever ye do, do it heartily, as to the Lord, and not unto men;* [24]*Knowing that of the Lord ye shall receive the reward of the inheritance: for ye serve the Lord Christ.* [25]*But he that doeth wrong shall receive for the wrong which he hath done: and there is no respect of persons.*

Below are three key points about relationships:

1. Relationships begin by putting God First
2. Relationships matter
3. Relationships take time, sacrifice and hard work

Fulfilling My Needs Will Make Me Happy

Have you ever met someone who just appears to be full of them-selves? It's all about them, and if their needs are not met, they become the most unhappy people in the world. It's as if the world is coming to an end. You get drama after drama all centered around what you are not doing to meet their needs. People are not meant to be our lives, they are meant to share and experience our lives with us. We are not to live our lives depending on others for approval, affirmation, purpose, safety or identity. This is a very vulnerable and unstable position to be in; where one individual believes that they can change another individual. Angel was willing to move to California to be with Tim who made no commitment to their relationship while he was pursuing his dreams.

So many singles become a victim of this lie. I need someone in my life to fulfill me. I need someone to make me happy. This scenario is heard time after time as young girls become pregnant with hopes of holding on to their lovers. Anything goes and anyone will do is the mindset of these young girls, just as long as they feel needed. Heartbreak is inevitable in these relationships as respect is not a criteria.

Being complete is not something that we quickly become; it is a journey. On this journey, we learn to rely on God, heal past hurts, unveil our masks and take control of our destiny.

There has been times during my hurts or valley experiences that I can recall wanting to quickly get past the pain. The passing of my father at the age of 40 years old is one of that quickly comes to mind. I remember having the most difficult time grieving because this process shook the very foundation I stood on and brought to surface so many repressed feelings. A counselor, Carolyn helped me make sense of this very dramatic time in my life. She helped me see that I was not losing touch with reality, but I needed to deal with my losses and past insecurities or they will resurface at another time of crisis. I had to deal with past hurts and losses to find peace stability and hope. Sigmond Freud talked about the Pandora box. This makes sense to me because I dug deep, endured pain and discomfort to find the missing buried pieces of my life, the key to hope.

Getting beyond the pain requires being transparent, not covering up but taking off the mask. Our mask is somewhat like a protective shell on a turtles back. It covers and also keeps us protected. We can appear and disappear at times of danger or vulnerability. It gives us a place to hide and feel safe.

The journey to experiencing healthy relationships requires what we do and what we say to match the real person that's on the inside. And It all starts with becoming transparent and developing Trust.

True freedom comes from understanding who we really are. Could there be people in this world, in their attempt to please others, find themselves living an entire life in prison always dreaming and never achieving. Everything in life requires planning. We must set goals or our journey through life will take us nowhere. Everyone who achieves a sense of true completeness in relationships learned to do four things:

1. Heal
2. Become transparent
3. Regain control
4. Rely on God

First, we must heal from past experiences of hurts. Past hurts can be painful to deal with, that is why we must put it behind us quickly to stop the pain. It is much easier to smile and pretend everything is okay than to run the risk of being transparent to and being asked the dreadful question, are you okay? No one wants to be transparent or reveal the dark places in their life. No one wants to be exposed to the world. The world can be a cruel place even though there are some good people in the world.

I remember going to the Verizon store to pick up an accessory for my mobile phone. It was late and I wasn't sure when the store closed. As I pulled up, I can tell that they were still doing business because there were customers inside. I quickly got out of the car and ran towards the store misjudging how high the pavement was. This happened so quickly. The next thing I knew I was sprawled out face down across the sidewalk. My face had landed on the grass side of the pavement. My knees and knuckles were burning and my shoes were off my feet. I was still clutching on to my pocketbook that helped me break my fall. As quickly as I went down, I got up totally embarrassed, I smiled, brushed myself off and avoided eye contact while going into the store. I remember a few people coming up to me saying; "Are you okay" I smiled and made light of it. I asked for a wet wipe to remove the itchy grass off my face and light blood on my knuckles. Amazingly enough, my knees were bruised but my stockings did not tear. I quickly put that experience behind me because it caused embarrassment and pain. This is not the story I am quick to share because there was nothing pleasant about that experience. So it is with our past hurts we quickly put our mask on and avoid dealing with the reality of the issues or problems until they resurface into bigger problems. We live with the scars, sometimes for life. I thank God through that experience that my injuries were not worse. The hope in all of that was that I fell but I did get up. I eventually went home, cleaned up and told my husband about it and laughed at the experience, which is something I could not do at the time.

Let's be real. It is not a good feeling to be rejected in the middle of hurt and pain. It makes the wound deeper and the healing process longer, which is why many would rather not deal with it.

We don't catch a sense of self worth from reading a book, attending a workshop, seeing a counselor or therapist. Self worth comes from hard work. I am an advocate for achieving the highest education possible and learning from others. But I must say that the reason why I am where I am today is because I have worked hard and remained focused on my dreams.

Second, we must remove our mask. Out mask is our protective shield, it protects us and gives us room to gradually reveal who we are or withdraw when our security is compromised. My personality is naturally to be an introvert. Growing up I was shy and could be found in my room reading when there was company around. I would do my share of entertaining our guest but only at my comfort level. Today, that is still my natural tendency. Even Though my professional, personal and spiritual roles require that I interact with hundreds of people at various settings. I prepare myself for those occasions but as soon as those responsibilities are over, I retreat to my world of quiet serenity.

The need to protect ourselves is so strong that we would much rather pretend for as long as it takes until our relationships prove to be safe. We fake it till we make it. What comes to mind is the turtle and the use of his hard protective shell. A turtle retreats at the slightest sign of danger. We must drop our mask and be real.

Third, we must take control of our lives. This step is very difficult. It gets easier with maturity. It's so easy to go through life being passive. This is where one does nothing but show up and let the process determine their destination. Most of us plan for a vacation more than we plan for our entire lives. Taking responsibility for our destiny also affects our relationships. To have healthy relationships we must have a true sense of identity. By taking control, we invite others to help us achieve our goals without feeling completely responsible for our success or failure. The tools necessary for reaching our destiny requires writing a vision statement of purpose and setting obtainable, meaningful goals. Our vision statement sets the course and our goals serve as our map guiding and leading us to our destiny. We can easily get off course if we follow a faulty map or overly ambitious goals of others so it's always good to go back to our vision statement to get back on course.

We must strive hard and stick to our plans in order for our goals to become a reality. To achieve a sense of completeness we must not only set goals but delay the desire for instant gratification. Delayed does not mean denied, good things come to those who persevere and wait.

The final step to completeness requires relying on God. God is our creator and we were created with a specific purpose. God also has an awesome plan for our lives and made us a promise that He would never leave us nor forsake us. God promises to order our steps and lead us down the path to our destiny. Our need for significance can interfere with our journey towards destiny. We search for success, wealth, position, prestige, beauty, and fame which ultimately lead us away from our most loving human relationships. Our significance cannot be found in things.

Earthly relationships will disappoint us, but our relationship with God will surely meet our deepest need for significance. God loves us unconditionally just the way we are even when others reject us or disappoint us. The word of God tells us that "God lives in us and His love is made complete in us. To be complete we must remember that only God's love makes us whole.

Family Rules, Roles, and Relationships

It is so true that "no other relationship shapes who we are more than our family. Most of what we think, feel, say and do is in response to the home environment we grew up in" Consciously or subconsciously we will make decisions to adopt or reject the life lessons we learned from our family. Some of the areas influenced are the career we choose, who we choose to marry the politics we support and the morals and values we live by. We learn life skills and knowledge that enables us to survive on our own outside our immediate family structure. Our families taught us many things, how to trust vs. how to distrust, how to speak up or how to stay silent, how to give and how to take, and how to express inappropriate feelings and how to express appropriate feelings. Our families play a key role in our lives because our family experiences set the standards for all other relationships.

Sometimes we find ourselves carrying emotional baggage. I remember an experience when I was in kindergarten that happened due to poor communication:

My uncle Cecil was coming to visit for the second time and he was given verbal directions to the house. Now he lives in the country where the use of transportation is not necessary, so he is used to walking miles to and from where he has to go. Well he utilized public transportation from Portland to Kingston, which was 4-6 hours drive. When he got to Kingston, he forgot how to get to the house but remembered where our school was. My sister and I both arrived at school together and went to our separate classes. She is younger and I am older. My uncle spotted my sister first and took her by the hand and asked her to show him the way home. I was called to the principal's office and was told that a man came in the school and grabbed my sister by the hand and kidnapped her.

One of her classmates told her classroom teacher. They immediately contacted my mom at work and the police department. My mom showed up at the principal's office within minutes and so did the police. We got in the car and went riding around the neighborhood hoping to spot my sister and her kidnapper. This was a very traumatic time in my life. I cried the entire time fearful that this man would harm my sister. I even wondered if I would ever see her again as we drove around for hours with no success. They took me to the police station and questioned me trying to fill in the blanks of when we left home to the time my sister was last seen. Mom gave them a description of my sister and the police drove us home. As we approached our home we saw my sister running around playing in the front yard and a man seated on the front steps. The police asked my mom is this the kidnapper? The police was ready to arrest him. My mother said, "Oh my God, that is my husband's brother from the country. We were expecting him sometime today." My mom was so angry that he did not use common sense by first getting permission from my mom and notifying the principal before taking my sister off the school premises. Maybe some other arrangements could have been made to find him a way home. That was not a good day in the life of our family because both my Mom and Dad were angry with my uncle. Emotional baggage can scar families and put a strain on relationships. Needless to say that was the last time I remember my uncle coming to visit us.

Learning begins at the very first stages in life and continues throughout childhood. The rules we learned from our families resulted from three reasons: The rules our families reinforced, the roles our families asked us to play and the relationships our families modeled for us.

Family Rules

Each of our families developed their own unique set of rules. Some rules are unspoken, yet embedded into the very fibers of our relationships. Both grandpas died and my grandma on my mother's side before I became a teenager. I remembered that both grandpas were tall and had a very distinguished looks. They both had great personalities, and there was never a dull moment when they were around. I think some of their strong spoken rules were:

- Go to school
- Get the best education available to you
- Finish what you start
- Always carry yourself well
- Live a happy balanced life
- Always help others
- Be supportive and loyal
- Make money

I never knew my grandma on my mother's side but my grandma on dad's side died when I was in my early twenties. So, I really did not learn as much from them as my mom. My mom's unspoken rules were:

- Be confident
- Know yourself
- Be kind to everyone
- Love God with all your heart
- Take care of your family
- Be loyal
- Be a hard worker
- When you fall, get up and move on

I have added a few spoken and unspoken rules of my own which I have learned in this process called life:

- Be complete in who you are
- Set goals and achieve them
- Don't move on to the next step until you have finished what you started
- Don't try to give more than what you have
- Keep a balanced life
- Love life and be happy
- Don't hang on to what you don't have
- Use wisdom, learn from past mistakes
- Appreciate the gifts and mentors God sends into your life
- Be devoted to your family

Family Roles

As families grow together each member's roles and responsibilities become a little clearer. Typically, the older children begin to accept the pressures and challenges of being the pioneers. A lot of weight is placed on each member's shoulder and the pressure gets more intense to fulfill that individual families roles and expectations. In so many families, their future is shaped by that individual families goals and expectations. In my family my oldest sister Joan, helped mom care for all five kids because she was the oldest. She felt the pressure after graduating from high school to get a job, which would start down the path of independence. She delayed opportunities to go to college until the latter part of her child rearing years. It was more of a challenge for her then because she had to balance so many hats, working studying and caring for her family.

Putting God First

Women today think men are so confusing and men today think women are so confusing. But what brings men and women together is God's purpose for our lives.

Romans 8:28 (KJV) ²⁸*And we know that all things work together for good to them that love God, to them who are the called according to his purpose.*

Relationships are the key to unlocking God's destiny and purpose for our lives. Our relationship with the Heavenly Father who gave us life guides us to our destiny.

God promised Abraham that through him all the nations (families) of the Earth would be blessed. Abraham was a Father, and in order for him to be a father, he had to have a son. And in order to have a son it had to come through his wife. So relationship was needed to fulfill God's promise.

So if we do what we are supposed to do, we will get where we need to go. Therefore every relationship requires:

- Putting "God First"
- Begins today and paves the way for tomorrow.
- Time, sacrifice and hard work.

People don't care how much you know until they know how much you care.

Paul gave us instructions that relationships begin at home in Colossians the 3rd chapter. When we lead well at home, we gain credibility to be heard in the marketplace (community).

Success is gaining the respect of those who know you best. Relationship matters just like life matters. There will be good relationships and bad relationships. What you do today will determine the kind of relationships you will have tomorrow. Relationships are a part of life's journey.

Relationships begin by putting God first.

John 3:16 For God so loved the world that he gave his only begotten Son.

We are to love and not control. We can't control other people's behaviors but we can control our own and trust God to help us establish good relationships.

Genesis described Eve when she came into the world perfectly at peace with her God and with her husband the only other person on the planet. She lived in paradise, possessing every pleasure imaginable. She never knew the meaning of embarrassment, misunderstanding, hurt, estrangement, envy, bitterness, grief, or guilt until she listened to her enemy and began to doubt God.

Her sorrow in life came about when she and her husband were banished from paradise and the presence of God because of disobedience to God. Her joy would be when Eve's off spring would eventually destroy the enemy.

When Adam and Eve sinned, they entered into a bad relationship with God and each other. When they heard God coming, they hid themselves. Sin causes a breakdown in our relationship with God, and consequently our relationship with each other. For man, this became the beginning of broken relationships.

But when we are in fellowship with God we are empowered to be in fellowship with each other. This happens as a result of the power of God's love.

Matthew 22:37-40 (KJV) [37] *Jesus said unto him, Thou shalt love the Lord thy God with all thy heart, and with all thy soul, and with all thy mind.* [38] *This is the first and great commandment.* [39] *And the second is like unto it, Thou shalt love thy neighbor as thyself.* [40] *On these two commandments hang all the law and the prophets.*

Our relationships are grounded in God.

In Genesis 2:18 says "It is not good for man to be alone."

Loneliness was the first thing that God said was not good for man. Two are always better than one, because they have a good return on their work. If one should fall down the other friend is there to help the other up.

Ecclesiastes 4:9-10 says, "But pity the man who falls and has no one to help him up."

What matters most in life is not what stairs we climb, what we own or have accumulated in life but what matters most are our relationships. Our creator knew the value of relationships. It is through relationships that He will change the world.

Healthy Vs Unhealthy Relationships

We have often heard many relationships speakers say that we need healthy relationships. Let's explore for a minute what that looks like.

Is it possible to live happily thereafter, love unconditionally and develop relationships that will last for a lifetime? Absolutely yes! This is not a fairy tale, but like everything in life this will require dedication and hard work. It will not be free from the challenges of life because those are ingredients for relationship growth.

We were created by God and given what we needed to survive the highs (healthy) and the lows (unhealthy) relationships. You might remember Bill Cosby a popular television celebrity. Well Bill found himself in one of those low places in life when he found himself in an affair. His wife Camile Cosby forgave Bill Cosby when he went public about the affair. She said they had been through so much together that she was not willing to give up on their love and relationship.

What Are Some Signs Of An Unhealthy Relationship?

- You find yourself suffering from low self esteem
  Due to verbal abuse in the relationship
- When you are with your friend you feel weak and insecure
- You feel sad, suspicious, angry and seriously deprived in the relationship
- You don't feel at liberty to share your feelings and problems with your friend
- There is no honesty in the relationship
- You spend more time feeling hurt than good due to mistreatment of each other

- You are always complaining about your relationship to others
- You are unable, and the other party is unwilling to solve conflicts together
- Your trust is constantly broken
- There is no enthusiasm about life because of the problems in the relationship
- When other areas of your life become affected by your brokenness in the relationship

We typically don't just wake up and find ourselves in the middle of a bad relationship. There have been so many signs along the way that was so easily ignored or brushed under the rug. Those signs were there all along we just did not give it the attention it needed.

What Are Some Signs Of A Healthy Relationship?

- There is a feeling of security and happiness when you are together or alone
- There is a feeling of fulfillment and excitement from each other about reaching goals and attaining dreams of becoming the best you both can be
- There is generosity and much love, that you desire to give everything you can to each other. You feel fulfilled in doing so to them and others

- There is a desire to please God and with the same devotion, loyalty and commitment please others

Vocabulary Words That Express Healthy Relationships

- Honor – To esteem each other highly, considering each other's needs and highly respecting each other
- Heart – This is a major organ in the body. Having heart means caring deeply for and nourishing each other through life
- Healing – Love wars cause injuries, it is true love that heals (repairs) the wounds allowing individuals to love again
- Honesty – Many married couples describe honesty as one of their most important basic needs
- Harmony – Two individuals blending and flowing together with the same rhythm. Like musical notes the individuals don't need to be the same but must blend harmoniously together as a duet
- Empathy – The ability to feel what your friend feels. Putting yourself in their place
- Equality – Respecting each other's opinions
- Empower – Supporting each other's feelings
- Energy – Strong chemistry that binds two together

- Agreement – Essential ingredient for developing trust. When trust is broken the relationship falls apart
- Appreciation – Admiration for each other
- Adaptable – Transitioning into change when necessary
- Acceptance – Approving and validating each other
- Listening – Paying close attention to what each other is saying
- Laughter – Laughter brings physical, emotional and psychological healing. Laughter is good for the soul
- Love – Holding each other dear and valuing the time spent together
- Loyalty – Being completely devoted to each other, being careful not to betray each other's feelings
- Trust – Feeling of safety with each other
- Talking – communication is key to a healthy relationship
- Thoughtfulness – Striving to truly understand each other
- Time – Sharing time together without other distractions

Let's stop and take inventory of what is important in your relationships. Take a few minutes to identify the three (3) most important things you value in your relationship prioritizing the most important first:

1._____
2._____
3._____

Acceptance	Flexibility	Openness
Admiration	Forgiveness	Passion
Appreciation	Friendship	Patience
Balance	Fun	Playfulness
Caring	Generosity	Politeness
Commitment	Gentleness	Reassurance
Common Interest	Gratitude	Respect
Communication	Honesty	Responsibility
Compromise	Individuality	Security
Compatibility	Integrity	Sensitivity
Fairness	Love	Sensuality
Family	Maturity	Sex
Shared Values	Supportiveness	Virtue
Shared-Experience	Tact	Warmth
Sincerity	Tolerance	Other_____
Stability	Trust	Other_____

How To Heal Broken Relationships

Most relationships that develop over time are based on agreements or contracts, I will do this if you do that, therefore it is no wonder they are easily dissolved. We don't ask much of casual relationships, but we demand a lot of serious relationships. These serious relationships have strong feelings attached and much time invested. Some relationships die because they are not moving forward. Some relationships die from neglect.

Types Of Broken Relationships

Irreconcilable differences:
- Unexpected change
- Starting a new relationship
- Growing apart

Betrayal:
- This broken relationship dismantles trust. When trust has been broken the relationship falls apart.

Ecclesiates 4:10 says, Woe to him who is alone when he falls and has not another to lift him up.

Step By Step Plan To Heal Broken Relationships

1. Count the cost
   a. Is your broken relationship worth repairing?
   b. What will it cost? My life, health or spiritual well-being?

2. Forge ahead
   a. If your relationship is worth repairing, make an effort to contact your friend. Keep your message simple. Stress the importance of how much you value the

relationship and that you want to resolve the conflict that stands between you.

3. Forgive
   a. It is very hard to let bygones be bygones. It is very hard to forgive. If you have been done wrong, it is hard to let go even if apologies were made. It is hard to turn the other cheek as the Bible instructs us to.

4. Identify the problem
   a. We find it hard to identify the problem for fear that the problem will be found in us. The last thing we want to do is admit that there is a problem. We want to point fingers at others but doesn't like having those fingers pointing back at us.

5. Rebuild Trust
   a. Once bitten twice shy. It is hard to put yourself in a position to be let down again. Trust is earned not deserved. You will definitely need God in your life to give you the strength to trust again.

The Healing Process

Getting beyond the pain requires being transparent not covering up but taking off the mask and revealing your inner self. Our mask is like a hard shield or a protective shell on a turtles back. Our mask shields us and keeps us covered and also keeps us protected. We can appear and disappear in times of danger or vulnerability.

Healing is a process that will not happen overnight, it will take time. You must make your relationship with God your first priority. Pursue opportunities for personal support and for the continual spiritual growth that God will make available to you along the pathway to healing. You will also need to develop healthy relationships and establish accountability with those you are in covenant relationship with.

As you begin to heal, God will open doors for you to share your experiences with others. God has a way of making all the things that happen in your life, (the good and the bad) work together for your good when you put Him first. God specializes in healing the broken hearted and setting the captive free. Experience the freedom and the joy, which comes from being whole from the inside out.

May the favor of God be upon your lives and upon your relationships! May you experience the richness of God as you allow others to enter into your life.

References

1. David G. Myers, the Pursuit of happiness (New York Avon Books, 1992).

2. Tori deAngelis, "A Nation of Hermits: The Loss of Community," The American Psychological Association Monitor (September 1995): 45-46.

3. Chip Walker and Elissa Moses, "The Age of Self- Navigation," American Demographics (September 1996): 38.

4. Bridget Murray, "College Youth Haunted by Increased Pressures," The American Psychological Association Monitor (April 1996): 47.

5. Ashley Montegue, "A Scientist Looks at Love," Phi Delta Kappa 11, no. 9 (May 1970): 463-67

6. David W. Smith, Men Without Friends (Nashville: Nelson, 1990), 46-47

7. J. Richard Stevens, Finding Faith in Faith Blog (October 3, 2004)

Resource and Contact Information

- To order other books and series by Pastor Wil and Dr. Grace Nichols

- To tune into "Victorious Talk with Pastor Wil and Dr. Grace"

- For booking information on Marriage and Relationship Seminars

- To receive an Inspirational Daily Word

Contact More Than Conquerors Publishing or Victorious Praise Fellowship Church of God in Christ:

Toll Free Number: 1-888-512-1895

Email: church@victoriouspraise.org

Website: www.victoriouspraise.org

Mailing Address: P.O. Box 14392
                 Durham NC 27709

Made in the USA
Middletown, DE
22 February 2021